GLOBETROTTER™

Travel Guide

KU-574-828

CANARY ISLANDS

ANDY GRAVETTE

NEW
HOLLAND

NH
NEW HOLLAND

★★★ Highly recommended
★★ Recommended
★ See if you can

This edition first published in 2000
by New Holland Publishers (UK) Ltd
London • Cape Town • Sydney • Auckland
First edition published in 1996
10 9 8 7 6 5 4 3 2 1

24 Nutford Place
London W1H 6DQ
United Kingdom

80 McKenzie Street
Cape Town 8001
South Africa

14 Aquatic Drive
Frenchs Forest, NSW 2086
Australia

218 Lake Road
Northcote, Auckland
New Zealand

Distributed in the USA by
The Globe Pequot Press
Connecticut

ISBN 1 85974 531 8

Although every effort has been made to ensure
accuracy of facts, telephone and fax numbers in this
book, the publishers will not be held responsible for
changes that occur at the time of going to press.

Commissioning Editor: Tim Jollands
Manager Globetrotter Maps: John Loubser
Editors: Thea Grobbelaar, Susannah Coucher,
Sara Harper
Picture Researcher: Emily Hedges
Design and DTP: Kathryn Fotheringham
Cartographer: Karen Bayley
Compiler/Verifier: Elaine Fick
Reproduction by Hirt & Carter (Pty) Ltd, Cape Town
Printed and bound in Hong Kong by Sing Cheong
Printing Co. Ltd.

Cover: *The colourful fishing boat harbour of Puerto
de Mogán, Gran Canaria.*
Title page: *Women in costume for Thanksgiving
at Betancuria, Fuerteventura, wearing the island's
characteristic pointed hat.*

CONTENTS

1
Introducing the Canary Islands

Basking in glorious year-round sunshine and surrounded by the aquamarine water of the Atlantic Ocean, each of the seven major Canary islands has its own unique charm. The majority of tourists flock to the endless strings of white sandy beaches, to enjoy the fabulous watersports and dance the night away in the high-energy clubs on Gran Canaria and Tenerife. Yet within minutes of the coast, even the most popular islands have a wealth of astonishing natural beauty, almost untouched by the modern world.

Gran Canaria is an exhilarating blend of old and new, backed by breathtaking scenery and with a cosmopolitan capital. **Fuerteventura** has spectacular sandy beaches with some of the best windsurfing conditions in the world. **Lanzarote's** haunting beauty is encapsulated in the eerie lunar landscape of Timanfaya National Park. The snow-capped peak of Mount Teide looms over **Tenerife's** lush vegetation. One of the world's largest volcanic craters dominates peaceful **La Palma**; **La Gomera** and **El Hierro** are even more tranquil. It is these contrasts that make the islands so appealing and it's easy to see why they're Spain's most popular holiday destination.

Each island is steeped in history, with a strong sense of individual identity. There's a fascinating local culture and the islanders happily welcome any new visitors. Whether your preference is for exploring and hiking, sightseeing or simply soaking up the glorious, hot sun, the choice is simply endless.

TOP ATTRACTIONS

*** Tenerife: Mount Teide National Park.
*** Lanzarote: 'lunar' landscape of Timanfaya Park.
** Fuerteventura: sandy beaches of Jandía peninsula.
** La Palma: the world's biggest volcanic crater, Taburiente.
** Las Palmas: the old Vegueta quarter of the city.
* La Gomera: Columbus's legacy in San Sebastián.
* El Hierro: the peaceful isolation of El Golfo bay.

Opposite: *The palm-fringed, golden sands of Playa Blanca, Lanzarote; a sun-lover's paradise.*

INTRODUCING THE CANARY ISLANDS

FACTFILE

Largest island: Tenerife 2046km² (790 sq miles).
Smallest island: El Hierro 277km² (107 sq miles)
Highest peak: Mount Teide on Tenerife is 3718m (12,198ft).
Government: Islands divided into two provinces, governor appointed by Spain.
Population: 1,830,000.
Most populated island: Gran Canaria (±720,000).
Least populated island: El Hierro (±8500).

Opposite: *At the summit of Mount Teide, Tenerife, the highest mountain in Spain.*
Below: *Caldera de Taburiente, La Palma, is an extinct volcano surrounded by snow-capped peaks and jagged pine trees.*

THE LAND

The Canary Islands consist of seven main islands and six minor ones in the Atlantic Ocean. From east to west, **Lanzarote, Fuerteventura, Gran Canaria, Tenerife, La Gomera, La Palma** and **El Hierro** are the major islands. The minor ones are Isla de Alegranza, Isla Montana Clara, Isla Graciosa, Isla de los Lobos, Roque del Este and Roque del Oeste. The islands are spun out over roughly 450km (280 miles) of the Atlantic, in an area covering 7500km² (2896 sq miles), just off the north-west coast of Africa. It is less than 96km (60 miles) from Fuerteventura to Morocco on the African mainland, and around 1120km (700 miles) northeast to Spain.

Although a long way south of Europe, the Canaries are still 480km (300 miles) north of the Tropic of Cancer. The average latitude of the Canaries is 28° North, and they lie between 13 and 18° west of the zero Meridian. For historical reasons the Canaries belong to Spain, but geographically they are part of **Macaronesia**, a volcanic island group which also comprises the Azores, Madeira and the Cape Verde Islands, all of which have similar topography and indigenous flora.

The Islands

The first Canary Islands, Fuerteventura and Lanzarote, were formed nearly 20 million years ago by giant volcanic eruptions. Gran Canaria was the next to emerge, followed by Tenerife and Gomera (about 12 million years ago) and then La Palma and El Hierro (two to three million years ago).

Although all the islands have a common volcanic origin, each has its own identity and character. Five of the islands are extremely mountainous and green: they are rocky, with deep valleys or *barrancos*, volcanic craters, thick forests and fertile plains. Fuerteventura and Lanzarote are bleak and arid, but also immensely interesting in their own right.

Tenerife is the largest island and covers 2046km² (790 sq miles). It is dominated by **Mount Teide**, which at 3718m (12,198ft) is the highest peak on Spanish territory. Next in size is Fuerteventura, covering 1730km² (668 sq miles). Gran Canaria, often termed a continent in miniature owing to its geo-

graphical diversity, covers 1533km² (592 sq miles) and is the most heavily populated, with over 650,000 inhabitants. Lanzarote's land area is 862km² (333 sq miles); that of La Palma 730km² (282 sq miles). Both La Gomera, which covers 372km² (144 sq miles) and El Hierro, the most westerly and the smallest island, with an area of 277km² (107 sq miles), are relatively unspoilt. The combined population of the Canary Islands is just under 1,500,000.

Seas and Shores

The deep **Atlantic Ocean** surrounding the islands abounds in fish such as cod, mackerel, sea bass, turbot and sardines. Sportsmen fish for bigeye, bluefin and long-tail tuna, marlin, swordfish and various types of shark. All types of shellfish, from lobster and prawns to oysters, litter the shallow pools around the islands' shores.

Climate

Canarios claim that their climate resembles springtime the whole year round. In fact, the southern sides of most islands can seem like a hot summer for most of the year, with cloudless skies and average **temperatures** of 25°C (78°F). The islands boast over 2500 hours of **sunshine** a year

VOLCANOES

The movement of the earth's crust, particularly the clash of continental plates, creates fissures in the thin surface of the globe, which allows molten magma to escape at high pressure. In some cases, the escaping lava may be forced up through a single volcanic cone, such as on Tenerife. This is how Mount Teide was created. Volcanoes can erupt at any time: the last volcanic eruption in the Canaries occurred on La Palma in 1971, when Teneguia exploded. A new landscape was created on Lanzarote from 1730, when a six-year period of volcanic eruptions began, leaving the molten magma just centi-metres below the surface.

CANARY ISLANDS	J	F	M	A	M	J	J	A	S	O	N	D
AVERAGE TEMP. °C	18	18	18	19	20	22	24	24	24	25	21	19
AVERAGE TEMP. °F	64	64	64	66	68	72	75	75	75	77	70	66
% HUMIDITY	67	67	66	64	63	62	59	60	65	68	69	67
HOURS OF SUN DAILY	6	8	7	7	8	10	10	8	6	6	5	5
DAYS OF RAINFALL	18	7.5	6	4.9	4	2	1	1	1	2	6	10
RAINFALL mm	36	8	2	11	2	0	0	0	6	3	58	9
RAINFALL in	1.5	0	0	0	0	0	0	0	0	0	2	0

EUPHORBIAS AND MORE

Similar to the Dragon Tree, the curious Euphorbia plant grows mainly in old lava flows and dates back to prehistoric times. Rather like a fleshy plantain, it contains a poisonous sap. Legend has it that the native Guanches poured small quantities of this sap into water in order to stupefy fish, and therefore making them more easy to catch. There are two types of this spurge-like plant on Lanzarote, the pale green *Euphorbia balsamifera*, and *Euphorbia obtusifolia*, called *tabaiba*, plus *Euphorbia canariensis*, a tall, cultivated, cactus-like plant, known locally as *cardon*.

Below: *The Euphorbia plant, indigenous to the islands, grows mainly in old lava flows and contains a poisonous sap.*

and during summer midday temperatures can reach a high of more than 32°C (89°F). When there is **rain** it falls between October and May. It can be **windy** in the summer when the *alisio* blows in from the northwest, and during the autumn the dust brought in by the *sirocco* directly from the Sahara Desert often forms a haze over the islands. **Snow** often lingers on the peak of Mount Teide until May.

Plant Life

You only have to wander through one of the islands' botanical gardens to appreciate the fabulous diversity of flora which abounds in the Canaries. The special climate and generally fertile soil provides ideal conditions. Most striking of the native species is the strange, primeval **dragon tree**, with its dagger-like leaves, which lives for many hundreds of years. Other native plants to look out for include the Canary date palm, Canary pine, gorse, tree ferns and laurelwood.

Spanish settlers brought their favourite plants, vegetables and fruit to the Canaries and, more importantly, **sugar cane** from the Far East. First introduced in the early 1400s, sugar cane became the islands' leading crop and remains a significant export to this day.

From the 15th century onwards the Canaries have been a stopping-off point for ships from around the world, whose crews have introduced numerous tropical fruits and flowers to the islands. The prettiest imported plants include oleander, bougainvillea, strelitzia (bird-of-paradise) and hibiscus. Today the food index of the islands reads like a botanist's tour of the world. Bananas, oranges, potatoes, tomatoes and flowers are important export crops, and the islands' grapes provide the world with the celebrated malmsey wine. On the drier islands, cacti and succulents such as prickly pear are widespread.

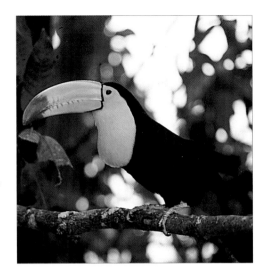

Above: *Keel-billed toucan, one of the exotic exhibits at Palmitos Parque, Gran Canaria.*

Wildlife

Many species of migratory birds use these isolated landfalls on their Atlantic wanderings. Apart from the common varieties of birdlife, there are curlew, egrets, hoopoe, sandpipers, oyster catchers, and the great grey shrike, or 'butcher bird'. There are many rare birds endemic to the islands, such as the **Fuerteventuran houbara**, the **chat**, the **Canarian buzzard**, the **blue chaffinch** and the common *Serinus canarius* – the **canary**, which was named after the islands. Altogether there are 70 resident species of birds on the islands, with around 200 visitors.

There are no large mammals, poisonous snakes or scorpions on the islands. The **Hierro giant lizard**, the **Canarian oyster catcher** and the **laurel pigeon** are all endangered species indigenous to the Canary Islands.

Some sheep and goats can be seen wandering on pasture land, plateaux, scrubland, and on valley floors, but there are few large herds of domesticated beasts. The local dog, known as a **verdino** because of its greenish tinge, is commonplace, and donkeys are often used as beasts of burden.

SHIPS OF THE DESERT

One of the surprising sights on the Canary Islands is the camel. Not indigenous to the islands, dromedaries (one hump instead of two) were probably brought to Lanzarote from Africa in the 15th century. They are used as beasts of burden and for transport. The camel's diet of thorn scrub and other plants of the *malpais* (badlands) is amply provided on Lanzarote; camels generally have a life expectancy of about 25 years.

Below: *Statue of an idealized Guanche chieftain; relics of this Stone Age race can be found throughout the islands.*

HISTORY IN BRIEF

The earliest inhabitants of the Canary Islands belonged to two racial types. Remains of **Cro-Magnon Man** (characterized by broad faces and high foreheads), dating from 3000BC, have been found on the islands. From around the same time a tall, blond-haired, fair-skinned race called **Guanches** also inhabited most of the islands.

Strictly speaking, the word *Guanche* means 'son of Tenerife' in the original island language – the Bimbache tribe lived on El Hierro and the Benahorita on La Palma – but the term is now used generically to describe ethnic Canarians who occupied the islands before the Spanish conquest. No-one has discovered when, or how, they came to the islands but, due to their lack of knowledge regarding boat-building and metals, it must have been at least 2000BC, before the Bronze Age.

Ancient Canarian society was **Stone Age** but not entirely primitive: they had a relatively sophisticated social structure. This varied from island to island, but most were divided into chiefdoms, ruled by a chief who was in turn advised by a council of elders.

Early visitors to the islands included **Phoenicians**, **Carthaginians** and the **Romans** but, as far as we know, no trading links or cultural contacts were established with the locals.

Spanish Conquest

Little seems to be known about the islands until the Genoese explorer Lanzarotto Malocello arrived in 1312 and gave his name to Lanzarote. Both Portugal and Spain sent ships to investigate the Canaries, and in 1344 Pope Clement VI installed the Spaniard Luis de la Cerda as King of the Isles. From then on, a succession of so-called 'kings' were appointed who ruled mostly *in absentia*, having little impact on the islands, whose native inhabitants were probably unaware they were being governed by anyone else. But in 1401 the Canaries were incorporated into the Castilian (Spanish) crown and then the

European conquest of the islands began with
a vengeance. In 1402 a Norman, Baron Jean de
Béthancourt, and a Spanish nobleman, Gadafir de la
Salle, took Lanzarote for the King of Castile. By 1406
they had captured Fuerteventura and La Gomera, but
failed to gain more territory in the face of fierce native
resistance on the other islands.

For around a century, the native tribes held off the
Spanish, who were also dogged by territorial disputes
with the Portuguese. In 1477, however, Portugal ceded
part of the Canary Islands to Spain and phase two of the
Spanish conquest leapt into action. Spanish conquistadores befriended some chiefs and annihilated others.
By 1483 Gran Canaria had been conquered and **Pedro
de Vera** was appointed as the first Spanish governor
of the Canaries. The other islands were captured in
swift succession. Tenerife, the last island to fall, was
conquered by **Alonso Fernández de Lugo** in 1494 after
ferocious fighting. Of the ethnic population, thousands
were enslaved, while many intermarried with Spanish settlers or fell victim to European diseases. By the end of the
16th century the ancient Canarians were all but extinct.

WHAT'S IN A NAME

The designation '**Isla
Canaria**' appeared for the
first time on a Spanish map
in 1339, but no-one knows
for certain how the islands
got their name. In Ancient
Greece they were termed
the '**Fortunate Isles**'. Pliny
the Elder (AD23–79) described
an expedition, made about
50 years before his time,
from the Roman colony
of Mauretania, relating the
name Canaris to the island
we now know as Gran
Canaria. Whether this name
originates from the Latin
for dog (canis), since there
certainly were dogs on the
island, or whether it comes
from the name canora for
singing bird (which might
have been on the island)
is anybody's guess!

HISTORICAL CALENDAR

3000BC–AD1500 Islands inhabited by Stone Age people;
origins unknown.
1100BC Phoenicians and
Carthaginians visit the islands.
1st century AD Expedition
from Roman colony of
Mauretania to the islands.
1312 Genoese explorer
Lanzarotto Malocello
names Lanzarote.
1340 Portugal and Spain send
ships to investigate islands.
1344 Pope Clement VI
appoints Spaniard, Luis de
la Cerda, King of the Isles.
1401 Canary Islands are
incorporated into the
Spanish Crown.
1402–1406 Gadafir de la Salle

and Jean de Béthancourt occupy
Lanzarote, Fuerteventura
and El Hierro.
1478 Captain Réjon founds
Las Palmas, Gran Canaria.
1483 Pedro de Vera appointed as first Governor of the
Canary Islands.
1492 Columbus visits
Canaries. Volcanic eruption
on Tenerife.
1494 Tenerife is the last
island to fall to Spain.
16th–17th centuries: Spanish
settlers establish thriving
economy using slave labour
1657 Admiral Blake attacks
Spanish treasure fleet.
1731 6 years of volcanic
eruptions begin on Lanzarote.

1797 Nelson attacks port
of Santa Cruz de Tenerife.
1852 Isabella II declares
Canaries a Trade Free Zone.
c1900 Bananas replace sugar
cane as mainstay of the
islands' economy.
1927 Canary Islands divided
into two provinces.
1936 General Franco plots
military coup on Tenerife.
1971 Volcanic eruption on
La Palma (the most recent).
1982 Regional constitution
granted by Spain to the
Canary Islands.
1986 The Canary Islands
achieve special status
within the European
Economic Community.

CHRISTOPHORO COLOMBO

Above: *The 15th-century explorer Christopher Columbus, who embarked from the Canary Islands on his epic 1492 voyage of discovery to the New World.*

CHRISTOPHER COLUMBUS

While the last desperate battles for control of the Canary Islands were being fought, Christopher Columbus stopped at the islands to refit his ships while on his voyage of discovery in search of a new sea route to the Indies in 1492. Columbus returned to the islands on subsequent trips. There are several monuments to Columbus on the islands and the elaborate **Casa de Colón** in Las Palmas has many contemporary exhibits.

Spanish Colonialism 1500–1800

The 16th century saw a vast influx of Spanish colonists who used Guanche slave labour in order to establish a profitable economy. The islands rapidly gained economic importance through the cultivation of sugar cane, introduced from Asia, which soon became the island's main source of revenue. Later, wine was to become an economic mainstay. Following Columbus's discovery of the New World in 1492, the islands became a vital staging post for ships, settlers and slaves on their way to and from the Americas.

From the time the Spanish first put their stamp on the islands, however, they became a target for not only the competing navies of **Britain** and **Portugal** but also for a cross-section of marauding pirates. For several hundred years the islanders were besieged by sea-borne attackers: the notorious **Barbary** pirates and **corsairs** conducted hit-and-run raids on the islands. During the 17th and 18th centuries the British, Dutch and Portuguese made many attempts to take the Canaries but were beaten off.

Even the land itself seemed to resent the colonists. During the 1700s, volcanoes erupted with frightening regularity. In 1731, seismic disturbance began on Lanzarote and lasted six years, transforming the land into an eerie moonscape. However, undeterred by harassment from the sea and the ravages of nature, the islanders took to political in-fighting to prove their dominance over one another.

Factionalism and Free Trade 1800–1900

Both **Gran Canaria** and **Tenerife** squabbled over which was to become the dominant island. The Canaries also took on the might of the mother country, Spain, in order to establish their identity. Even now the islanders deny that they are Europeans, stating that they are African. Certainly the islands are much nearer the African mainland than they are to Madrid.

The in-fighting resulted in the eventual establishment of a Permanent Island Council, or *cabildo*, of Gran Canaria in Las Palmas in 1808. From this time, the *cabildo* system became adopted throughout the islands, each appointed from mainland Spain and responsible for administering their own separate affairs. Las Palmas became the capital of Gran Canaria in 1820, but Santa Cruz de Tenerife was established as the capital of the whole archipelago in 1822. The Canaries were declared a **free-trade zone** (duty-free) in 1852 by Isabella II in order to stimulate the economy. The development of the harbour of Las Palmas was begun in 1882 and by the end of the century, bananas had replaced sugar as the islands' main crop.

From the middle of the 19th century, a new invasion had begun, that of **tourism**. It coincided with the advent of the steamship and when the routes to and around South Africa were established. Visitors arrived in the Canaries by boat from Western Europe, beginning an influx of tourists which was only halted during the two World Wars. There were, however, several hiccups in the political stability of the islands which interrupted the tourist trade, particularly towards the end of the 19th century, when the examples of **Filipino** and **Cuban** insurrection against Spanish rule stirred Canario patriotism.

NELSON'S ARM

Lord Horatio Nelson was a 38-year-old admiral when he led a landing party of English marines in 1797, attacking Santa Cruz de Tenerife. Grapeshot raked his gallant band, and the heavy fire drove the British back to their ship, the *Theseus*, which was moored out in the bay.

A total of 226 British sailors were killed in the fray, and another 123 wounded. When the survivors carried Nelson on board they noticed that his right arm was badly damaged. It had to be amputated. The tattered flags that Nelson's contingent carried into battle now hang in the parish church of Santa Cruz and in the Paso Alto castle is the cannon, the *Tiger*, that fired the telling shot at Nelson's arm.

Left: *Banana plantation, Tenerife. By the end of the 19th century, bananas had become the islands' most important cash crop.*

Above: *Over the years, the Canary Islands have built up a chain of luxurious accommodation, including this parador in Teide National Park, Tenerife.*

A TENUOUS NEUTRALITY

Both Spain and the Canary Islands remained neutral during the two world wars. While maritime traffic dropped off during both periods, there are rumours that **General Franco** had secret dealings with the Germans during **World War II**, giving almost the entire Jandía peninsula to a German engineer. Stories abound of night landings of German submarines and underground bunkers. It was from these positions that the Nazis were supposed to have preyed on Allied shipping.

The 20th Century

Before the outbreak of World War I the Canary Islands were still strategically important as a stopping-off point in the Atlantic seaways, but war seriously interrupted the islands' trade. This was followed by an exodus of islanders to the New World.

The islands were divided into two provinces in 1927: the **Western Islands**, governed from Tenerife, and those ruled from Gran Canaria, the **Eastern Islands**. In 1936, **General Francisco Franco**, military governor of the Canaries, planned a military coup in Spain while on Tenerife, which eventually led to the formation of a Spanish Republic. During the **Spanish Civil War**, and continuing through Franco's dictatorship (1936–1975), the Canary Islands were largely neglected by Spain and by the world's tourists. The importance of the Canaries as a stepping-stone to the New World and the Far East declined with the advent of aircraft and the opening up of the **Suez Canal**. Tourism, however, took off again during the 1960s, quickly becoming the islands' main source of convertible revenue, as incoming visitors increased from a few thousand to the several million who are now welcomed each year .

GOVERNMENT AND ECONOMY

System of Government

The Canaries are part of Spain, a country that hashad
a constitutional monarchy since 1978. The islands
consist of two provinces which since 1982 have been
one autonomous region (there are 17 altogether in
Spain), responsible for self-government. Spain is part
of the European Union.

The seven main islands in the archipelago have
comprised two of Spain's 50 provinces since 1927.
Las Palmas Province is made up of Gran Canaria,
Fuerteventura and Lanzarote; **Santa Cruz de Tenerife
Province** comprises Tenerife, La Palma, La Gomera and
El Hierro. Both provinces have civil and military gover-
nors appointed from Madrid. The **Gobinero de Canarias**
(Government of the Canaries) is responsible for all
domestic Canarian matters such as health services,
roads and water supply. Each island is divided into
smaller administrative units (*municipios*). There has
always been friction between the seven Canary Islands
governing bodies, especially between Tenerife, now the
capital of the Western Islands, and Gran Canaria, the
capital of the Eastern Islands.

Above: *The Canary
Islands' flag, adopted in
1982 when the islands
became an autonomous
region. The colours were
taken from the naval flags
of Santa Cruz de Tenerife
and Las Palmas.*

Below: *Volcanic soils
on Lanzarote are fertile;
here, workers gather the
onion harvest at La Haria.*

The **Union of the
Canarian People** and the
more radical **Movement
for Self-Determination
and Independence** are
both pressurizing for total
independence from Spain.
This is not supported by
the majority of the people.
Instead, many Canarians
feel Spain should eco-
nomically support their
islands, as they put the
blame for their poverty
on Spain's neglect of the
Canaries during General
Franco's dictatorship.

Economic Development

The economy of the islands rode a stormy sea for many hundreds of years. The ravages of nature, particularly the many volcanic eruptions, famine and regular attacks by pirates, dogged the Canaries' early prosperity. The fertile black soil and an equable climate, however, made for an ideal agricultural environment. At one time, the islands' economy was almost entirely based on sugar, wine, tomatoes, bananas and cochineal.

Today, bananas, tobacco, coffee, potatoes, tomatoes, avocados, dates and citrus fruits, vines and carpets of flowers thrive in the near perfect climate. However, because the subsidies to banana-growers in Central America and the Caribbean have lowered the price of the fruit, many banana farmers are turning their attention more to lucrative crops such as exotic vegetables, flowers, pot plants and pineapples

Industry

With their proximity to the European mainland and the plethora of cheap charter flights, the Canary Islands represent one of the most convenient destinations for travellers seeking year-round sun, sand and sea.
Tourism is now shaping the islands' future: indeed, some islands depend on its revenue. There are airports on six of the seven major islands and one is under construction on La Gomera. New roads have opened up the wealth of scenery which abounds throughout the Canaries. Today the islands are a mecca for tourists from Germany, Scandinavia, Britain, and mainland Spain. Of the 43 million tourists who visit Spain annually, the Canaries attract almost a quarter of that number alone.

Below: *The black sandy beach of Playa de la Arena, Tenerife, a year-round holiday destination.*

THE PEOPLE

Today's Canarios are a proud, friendly and easy-going people, willing to help and delighted to show visitors their culture and countryside. They are fiercely *Canarios* rather than *Peninsulares*, which is what they call the Spanish. Having been a bridge between Europe and the rest of the world for so long, there is a great ethnic mix of people who are fully integrated into society. Each islander has his own indentity within the Canary Islands. Those from Gran Canaria are known as **Canarios**; the people on Fuerteventura are called **Fuerteventurans** and those on Lanzarote, **Lanzarotenos**. On Tenerife the people are **Tinerfeños**; on Palma, **Palmeros**; on La Gomera, **Gomeros**; and on El Hierro, **Herreños**. Evidence of intermarriage between early colonists and **Guanches** is still evident in the features of many islanders today.

Illiteracy is still a problem on the islands: at the end of Franco's dictatorship it was estimated to be as high as 50% in some rural areas and stands at between 7–10% today, far higher than on mainland Spain. Society is also changing rapidly due to worker migration from the villages to the resorts.

Above: *Tinerfeños in traditional dress: bright colours and geometric designs are a Guanche legacy.*

Language

The universal language in Spain is **Castilian Spanish** (textbook Spanish), but the dialect used on the Canary Islands is more like that of Latin America. The last 's' in a word is often not pronounced. A 'z' is not pronounced *th* as in Spain, but as an *s*. A 'c' before 'i' or 'e' is pronounced *s*. Words are often curtailed, and are sometimes run together in a sentence, making the individual words difficult to understand.

Many **Guanche** words have remained, particularly in place names. These often begin with the letters 'gua', which is pronounced *wah*. Coincidentally, this prefix

---

THE CANARIO

The typical Canario male is a caricature unto himself. In the Canarian writer, Pancho Guerra's stories, his name was Pepe Monagas, his wife Camildita. The island's sugar, rum and food gave him a large stomach, around which he would traditionally wear a wide sash and where a special local knife would protrude. A loose shirt would be covered by an open waistcoat, and, on his head, the archetypal Canarian would wear a battered old hat. Below baggy trousers, he would wear a pair of ill-fitting boots. Today, the only remnant of the Pepe figure is in the language and the macho moustache with the cigar stub. On festive occasions the Canarios wear distinctive costumes, varying from island to island.

occurs frequently in the Cuban language and can be traced back to the pre-Columbian days of the **Taino Amerindians**. A typical Cuban import is the name for the local buses – 'gua-gua', pronounced *wah-wah*.

Local patois or dialects are heard on some islands and in the countryside. It is perhaps better for the visitor to avoid trying to learn the local dialect and to stick to mainland Spanish, although English, and most western European languages, are widely understood. Outside the main towns and resort areas, it's a good idea to carry a small dictionary or phrase book.

Religion

Although pagan for many thousands of years under the ancient Guanche civilization, the conquering Spaniards brought **Roman Catholicism** with them to the islands. It is now the dominant religion. There are numerous churches dotted throughout the islands. However, there are Anglican and other denomination churches, a couple of synagogues and a mosque. Times of services are usually announced in Spanish and English outside most churches and visitors should observe these times when visiting the islands' historic churches.

El Silbo

The unique whistling language of La Gomera, *el silbo*, is legendary, invented for communications over long distances of difficult terrain, most probably by the native Guanche population. Apparently the *silbadores* can be understood up to 8km (5 miles) away. It is still in use today and fishermen and farmers find it very handy for keeping in touch with each other while out of sight at sea, or on the steep-sided fields. A good place to hear the silbo is in the grounds of Gomera's only parador, where gardeners use it to communicate with each other.

Canary Island Festivals

Fiestas (festivals) are the traditional method for celebrating saints' days and religious occasions. Most fiestas are of a religious nature, and each island has its own patron saint. **Candelaria** is the patron saint of the Canary Islands as a whole and the patron saint of Spain is **Santiago**, or St James. Don't miss the festival of **Corpus Christi**, when islanders spend painstaking hours making carpets of sand and flowers, or **Carnaval** (Carnival), which rivals that of Rio de Janeiro. September's **Santísimo Cristo** fiesta is spectacular, with fireworks and folk dancing, and Las Palmas' pilgrimage of **Nuestra Señora de la Luz** includes a procession of boats. There are numerous festivals throughout the islands, each one an enchanting mix of local culture, spectacle and tremendous fun.

Fiestas can also take the form of pilgrimages (*romerías*) and agricultural parades, accompanied by satirical songs (*murgas*). Many of these celebrations are visual feasts, with participants dressed in fabulous costumes and plazas decorated in bunting. Some of the most stunning decorations are the floral carpets which you can see at **La Orotava** and **La Laguna** on Tenerife,

and the sand, grass, pebble and flower patterns around
the cathedral in **Las Palmas**. Each island, city, town and
village seems to have its own patron saint. Certainly the
Canarian joke of a fiesta happening somewhere in the
islands every day seems to ring true!

Firework displays, horse parades, bonfires, parades of
religious statues and icons, traditional folk dancing and
ritual enactments are all part of the fiesta fun. In addi-
tion, fiestas often mingle pagan customs and religious
elements – a reminder of the long-standing dependency
of the islanders on nature. A number of these celebrations date back to the dark, mysterious times of the
Guanches. These include the **Rain Fiesta** of Telde and
the **Rama Fiesta** of Agaete on Gran Canaria. Often local
historical events are incorporated in the religious festivi-
ties, like the re-enactment of the repulsing of **Sir Francis
Drake** from Fuerteventura and Gran Canaria, or the
two-century-old ritual of beating off swarms of locusts
which once threatened crops in Guia, Gran Canaria.

Carnivals give the islanders yet another opportunity
to let their hair down. These generally do not have any
religious significance, being mainly a social event for
the local community to enjoy the parades, stalls and folk
dancing. *Ferias* (town fairs) are also a popular diversion,
often held in conjunction with the local carnival.

Right: *Revellers make
final adjustments to their
appearance before the Mardi
Gras parade, Tenerife.*
Opposite: *Religious
procession in Santa Cruz
de la Palma passing by
the replica of Columbus's
ship, the* Santa María.

Sport and Recreation

There are some unique Canarian sports and pastimes which date back thousands of years, at least to the days of the Guanche civilization, if not further. **Canarian wrestling**, or *lucha canaria*, which was developed by the ancients, is famous throughout the world and its rules are strict and rigid. Teams generally consist of two league teams of 12 *luchadores* (participants). Two barefoot contestants stand inside a 10m (33ft), sand-covered circle, in a stadium called a *terrero*, and attempt to throw each other to the ground. Individual bouts are known as *bregas*. Judging is complicated and requires much debate before a decision is declared by the judge. Canarian

MAJOR FESTIVALS

5 January Procession of the Magi: Santa Cruz de Tenerife and Las Palmas de Gran Canaria.
January–February Canary Islands Music Festival: Las Palmas de Gran Canaria and La Orotava, Tenerife.
February–March Gran Carnaval: Las Palmas de Gran Canaria, Santa Cruz de Tenerife and Puerto de la Cruz. Winter Festivals (Sixth week before Palm Sunday) Las Palmas de Gran Canaria.
March–April Holy Week: Las Palmas de Gran Canaria, Santa Cruz de Tenerife and La Laguna Tenerife. Opera Festival: Las Palmas de Gran Canaria and Santa Cruz de Tenerife.
29 April Royal incorporation of Gran Canaria into Castilian Crown: Las Palmas.
April–May Spanish Festivals of theatre, ballet, music etc: Las Palmas de Gran Canaria and Santa Cruz de Tenerife.
May Spring Festivals and Opera: Santa Cruz de Tenerife.
1–5 May Founding of Santa Cruz de Tenerife.

20 May San Isidro Labrador Festival: Los Realejos, Tenerife.
30 May Canary Islands regional holiday. Corpus Christi Floral carpet festival: Las Palmas de Gran Canaria, La Laguna, Tenerife, and Villa de Mazo, La Palma. Octava de Corpus La Orotava, Tenerife.
21–30 June (every five years) Nuestra Señora de las Nieves Festival: Santa Cruz de la Palma.
21–30 June (every four years) Nuestra Señora de las Nieves Festival: Valverde, El Hierro.
First Sunday of July San Benito Abad Festival: La Laguna Tenerife
14 July San Buenaventura Festival: Betancuria, Fuerteventura.
16 July La Virgen del Carmen Festival: Santa Cruz de Tenerife.
25 July Santiago de Apostol, Gáldar and San Bartolomé Festival and Defence against Nelson's attack: Gran Canaria and Santa Cruz de Tenerife.
5 August Virgen de las Nieves Festival: Santa Cruz de la Palma and Agaete, Gran Canaria.

16 August San Roque Festival: Garachico, Tenerife.
25 August San Gines Festival: Arrecife, Lanzarote.
28 August San Agustin Festival: Arafo, Tenerife.
6–8 September La Virgen de Pinto Festival: Teror, Gran Canaria.
7–15 September El Santisimo Cristo Festival: La Laguna, Tenerife.
11 September El Charco Celebrations: Aldea de San Nicolas, Gran Canaria.
Sunday after 17 September El Cristo del Calvario Festival: Icod de los Viños, Tenerife.
12 October Celebration of Columbus's discovery of America in 1492.
Second Saturday in October Nuestra Señora de la Luz Festival – (best procession): Las Palmas de Gran Canaria.
November–December Opera Festival: Santa Cruz de Tenerife.
13 December Santa Lucia Festival: Gran Canaria.
26 December Canary Islands regional holiday.

Above: *Windsurfing, one of the many watersports to be enjoyed in the Canaries.*

wrestling is practised throughout the islands and is a popular tourist attraction, as well as a feature of most fiestas. To commemorate the history of Canarian wrestling, many matches are held at original Guanche strongholds. Historians have noted that Canarian wrestling is similar to that practised by the ancient Egyptians.

The other unique national sport is called *juego de palo*, or *banot*, the stick game. This is also said to date from Guanche times. It is rather like fencing but instead of using swords, contestants use long poles.

On Tenerife and La Palma, islanders specialize in a method of getting around in a land of deep ravines and rugged gorges. They employ a technique of pole-vaulting known locally as the *salto del regaton de la garrocha*, or **pike leap**. Here amazing feats are performed with the use of a pole of around 2.5m (6½ ft) in length. The contestants leap down the mountain sides with a skill derived from the ancient inhabitants of the island.

Canarios have a passionate love of cock-fighting and dog-fighting, which are not illegal on the islands. However, bullfighting has never been popular, unlike on the Spanish mainland.

The sea offers the tourist a great variety of wonderful sporting opportunities. A unique watersport is the *vela latina*, a yachting race involving short 'Optimist' boats with vast triangular sails. Races and regattas are held at most weekends wherever conditions are right.

Yachting, sailing, power-boat racing, water-skiing and **windsurfing** are popular pastimes throughout the islands. Because the sea temperature ranges from around 22°C (72°F) to 19°C (66°F), and the sea

---

WORLD RECORDS

Huge shoals of fish run the gauntlet of Canarian fishing boats especially between the islands of Fuerteventura and Lanzarote and mainland Africa. The attraction for visitors is the opportunity to try their hand at deep-sea fishing. No licence is required for this increasingly popular sport. Many world record fish have been caught off the islands' coasts. Swordfish, white marlin, blue marlin, bluefin, yellowfin and a tuna known locally as *atún de ojo grand*, are popular for weight records.

abounds in many interesting volcanic and coral formations, teeming with marine life, **scuba diving** and **snorkelling** are also extremely popular. Visibility in some waters can be up to 40m (130ft) and there are also several fascinating underwater national parks around the islands for the preservation of undersea life. The **Gulf Stream** which sweeps past the islands also brings in prize-winning fish, making **deep-sea fishing** a main attraction for devotees. Freshwater reservoir fishing is also possible on some islands, but a licence must be obtained first from the Ministry of Agriculture and Fisheries.

Other activity sports, apart from **hiking**, **rambling**, **walking** and **climbing**, include **mountain-biking**, **hunting**, **riding**, **tennis**, **squash**, **golf** and **soccer**, a favourite with Canarios. There are numerous dog tracks, horse-racing and show-jumping clubs and motor-rallying contests. The **El Corte Inglés** motor rally on Gran Canaria is internationally famous.

Food and Drink

Owing to the great influx of tourists to the Canaries, foreign cuisine abounds throughout the islands. There are restaurants, however, which not only serve traditional Canarian food, but also local dishes of the particular islands. Restaurants are graded with a 'fork' symbol: five forks being the best. Meals are generally light, being more digestible in a warm climate.

A variety of fresh vegetables, fruit and fish forms the basis of Canarian cuisine. The traditional island food is *gofio*, a kind of flour meal made from toasted cereals. *Gofio* is used to make the island's celebrated nougat and is often a substitute for bread. Another staple food is *papas arugadas*, small potatoes cooked in their skins with a lot of salt.

Below: *A mouth-watering variety of local dishes on offer at a food stall in Puerto de la Cruz, Tenerife.*

Above: *Locally caught fish drying in the sun on Lanzarote's northern coast.*
Above right: *Vegetables grow in abundance on the islands. Here, corn is hung out to dry.*

GOFIO

When Spanish colonists met opposition from the local Guanche tribes on Fuerteventura, their attempts at obtaining a forceful submission failed. They then hoped to employ the alternative weapon of starvation.

This also failed, as the local *majoreros* began cultivating an indigenous glasswort plant from which they produced a native meal, *gofio*. In the 16th century, Indian corn, or maize, was introduced as a substitute. This quickly became the island's traditional dish. *Gofio* is still a local island delicacy – made from a mixture of wheat and maize flour.

Dishes imported from Spain include small, tasty dishes of bite-size morsels known as *tapas*, *gazpacho* (cold soup) and *paella* (saffron rice with vegetables, meat and fish). Tenerife is famous for its spicy sauces such as *salsa mojo picon*, made from peppers, garlic and other hot ingredients. La Gomera specializes in *salsa verde*, featuring coriander and parsley, which is particularly good with fish.

Meat eaters will find rabbit (*conejo*), chicken (*pollo*), kid goat, or wild pork, often marinated in a sauce of vinegar, herbs and garlic (*salmorejo*). Stews (*puchero* or *estofado*) are commonplace in the Eastern Province, often eaten with *gofio*. *Potaje canariense* is a vegetable and tomato soup thickened with *gofio*. Other favourite traditional soups include *sancocho* (meat, potatoes and vegetables) and *sopa de berros* (watercress and herb soup). *Sopa de millo* is a thin maize and meat broth made with *gofio*.

Fresh **fish** is naturally always on offer. There's a mouthwatering variety of exotic and everyday fish, which is usually cooked plain – either grilled, boiled or fried. Fish casseroles (*cazuela canaria*) are universally popular. Particular fish to look out for include *la vieja*, *cherne* (stone bass), grouper, *corvina* and horse mackerel on Tenerife, and *tollo* on Lanzarote. Some islands serve *sancocho*, a fish salad with hot sauce.

Desserts usually include the delicious fruit, such as mangoes, paw paw, cherimoya and bananas. Hierro is renowned for its cheesecake (*quesadillas*) and La Palma for its almond cheese. Another delicacy includes *bienmesabe* which contains almond cream, egg and honey. *Tirijalas*, or *torrijas*, are sweet, maize-flour fritters soaked in syrup; *Frangollo* are sweet pancakes made from honey, almonds, raisins, milk and corn. *Platanos fritas* are fried bananas sprinkled with lemon juice, brandy and sugar – delicious.

El Hierro produces some of the most exquisite **cheeses**, made from a mixture of cow, goat and sheep's milk. *Queso Herreño* comes either smoked (*ahumada*), or mature (*curada*).

Drinks include rum, honey-rum (*ron miel*), **malmsey** wine and red wine (*vino tinto* from Tacoronte, Tenerife, is the most widely available). Rum and coke is known as *cubatas*. Coffee is an important produce on the Canaries and *cafe solo* is small, strong, sweet and black. *Cafe con leche* is milky coffee, often made with sweet condensed milk.

The Arts

The islands have been the cradle of many celebrated writers, artists and musicians. **José Eugenio**, the famous 18th-century goldsmith, was a Canario, and Guia, on Gran Canaria was the birthplace of the 18th-century sculptor, **José Lujan Pérez**. Las Palmas was the birthplace of novelist **Benito Pérez Galdós**. **Pancho Guerra,** the writer, was also a Canario. Local artist **Néstor de la Torre** launched a campaign to revive Canarian folk art and architecture, and designed the Canarian Village in Las Palmas. Architect, design guru and enviromentalist, **César Manrique** was Lanzarote's most famous citizen.

TAPAS

Tapas are a Spanish speciality and they come in a wonderful variety of tastes. These snacks consist of small pieces of fish, shrimp, octopus (*pulpo*), squid (*calamares*), shellfish, and meat, pork or goat, marinated in sauces (*mojo*), with a variety of small plates of side salads and olives. *Tapas* can also be small slices of *tortilla*, a flan, or omelette, with potatoes, onions and vegetables. *Ropa vieja*, literally 'old woman's clothes', is another popular *tapa*, and is a small bowl of thick stew.

Below: *A characteristically simple mural by the celebrated Canarian artist César Manrique at Tahiche, Lanzarote.*

CESAR MANRIQUE

Born in Lanzarote in 1920, César Manrique is the Canaries most celebrated artist. With a string of exhibitions and shows, Manrique turned his skills to building the powerfully contemporary **Monumento Campesino** in 1968. Other striking artistic additions to the Lanzarote landscape, installed by the artist, are the **Jamenos del Agua**, on the northeast coast, and the **El Diablo** restaurant in Timanfaya National Park.He was killed in a car crash in 1992.

MEDIA

You'll find several foreign-language newspapers aimed at tourists in the Canary Islands: the main ones are *Lanzarote Holiday Gazette* and *Island Connections* (Tenerife). Tourist offices, hotels and many bars have free guides listing what's on and where to go. All the main foreign newspapers are available in the towns.

Below: *The wooden balcony surrounding the second-storey windows of the basilica in Candelaria is a typical architectural feature designed to give extra shade.*

Secindino Delgado, the patriot and founder of the newspaper *El Guanche*, was born in the Canaries, as was the mother of José Marti, Cuba's national hero. **Miguel de Unamuno**, a Spanish poet exiled on the island of Fuerteventura in 1924, enthused over its landscape. Local musical groups such as **Los Majuelos**, the **Sabandenos** and **Taburiente** have quite a following world-wide.

The Canary Islands are home to a wealth of museums and art galleries, apart from the numerous churches which house collections of precious artwork. In Las Palmas the **Santa Ana Cathedral** has a wonderful museum of Aztec and pre-Columbian treasure, and most island capitals have fascinating museums packed with local treasures. On La Palma, a concrete replica of Columbus's ship, the **Santa María**, houses a Maritime Museum, as does the **Casa de Colón** in Las Palmas.

In La Orotava, Tenerife, the **Casa Tafuriaste** has one of the best collections of regional ceramics in all of Spain. In Valle Guerra, on Tenerife, the **Casade Carta Ethnological Museum** has a comprehensive collection of regional costumes, and the **Castillo San José**, in Arrecife, on Lanzarote, is the home of the Museum of Contemporary Art. Probably the best place to see a complete cross-section of Canarian art, crafts and culture is at the **Pueblo Canario Museum**, the model Canary Island village in Doramas Park, Las Palmas.

Architecture

Typical Canarian architecture encompasses a variety of styles. Round, stone dwellings, and almost inaccessible necropoli carved out of rock, stand as testament to the building skills of the ancients.

Modern, or western, architecture was brought by the Spanish to the islands. Spanish building design had been influenced by many hundreds of years of Moorish occupation. The Canary Islands are often bereft of water, co-incidentally an important factor in Spanish or Moorish house design. In early architecture, most houses were built around a central courtyard, or patio, focused on a well. The central well was so important that Moorish architects embellished the well with exotic and expensive tiles. This trend was carried on in the Canary Islands. Often rainwater was collected in butts or large stone jars from the roofs and ornate spouts can still be seen protruding from many roofs.

Given the climate, the Moorish building designs (a style which is known as *mudéjar*), were naturally adopted in the Canaries. Originally without any air-conditioning, it was essential to construct houses with an effective air flow, guaranteed by the ever-present patio, a central feature of Canarian architecture. Styles of architecture range from colonial Baroque, through Rococco, Victorian Gothic, to Art Nouveau and Art Deco, and to the modern and futuristic designs of Lanzarote architect **César Manrique**. They also reflect both the artistic styles of the Old and New World as several churches sport traditional Mexican designs, derived from the Spanish conquest of the Aztecs and Mayans.

Patios were usually filled with shady trees and surrounded on all four sides by a colonnaded cloister. In a typical old Canarian townhouse, protection from the heat of the sun and occasional rainstorms was paramount in colonial building design. Columned, covered walkways extending the length of the house frontage were also popular features, many of which can be seen in the grandiose palaces and early official residences on the plazas of the old squares. Cobbled streets, plazas and alleyways are another feature of colonial architecture, worn smooth over the centuries by boot leather, hooves, and the wheels of countless horse-drawn carriages.

Above: *Traditional Canarian buildings were designed to give protection from the sun.*

THE CANARIAN COURTYARD

Features of the enclosed courtyard are typical of many of the very early Cuban buildings. In order to increase the amount of shade in the cobbled courtyard, trees were often planted in strategic positions. A well often featured in the courtyard.

Later adaptations in courtyard design sometimes included terracotta spouts protruding from the gulleys of the roofs of the balcony, from which rainwater was caught in large vats.

Above: *Many architec-tural details reflect a Moorish influence.*
Below: *Folk dancing and traditional music are still very popular in the islands.*

PARALLELS WITH CUBA

Just over half a century ago, many islanders emigrated to the Caribbean, taking their skills and culture with them. Sugar, Cuba's main produce, was first planted on the island by Columbus, who brought the plant from the Canaries. Today, factories in the Canaries process much of Cuba's second product, tobacco. Experts are also now comparing the similarities between prehistoric Taino drawings or carvings found on Cuba with the rock paint-ings of the Guanche of the Canaries. The strategic loca-tion of the twin Free Ports of Las Palmas and Tenerife, compares in importance to that of Havana.

Many Canarian houses are dazzling architectural gems, with whitewashed walls and red-tiled roofs, surrounded by a wide patio and cloister-like roofing overhanging the main structure. A balcony usually runs around the inside of the building, overlooking the cobbled patio, and railed around with finely turned hardwood support, often of Cuban mahogany or Canarian laurel.

Typically, governor's palaces and grand villas were also designed to stay cool. Wide doors, opening out on to the patio, provided a through-draught of air, and high windows in the outside wall ensured excellent air-conditioning. The deep, long windows around the second storey, on the outside of the building, were enclosed on three sides by fretwork screens, copying the Moorish style. The windows could be closed from the inside with shutters. Under the second storey, long windows were topped by individual narrow, tiled roofs. These windows stood out from the wall of the house with their wooden fretwork screens and together with their tiled roofing and own screens, light and air flowed freely into the lower-floor rooms.

Music and Dance

This is the favourite Canarian pastime for celebrating. At every opportunity the islanders take great delight in per-forming their unique variations of both dance and song. The *timple*, only found on the Canary Islands and in Cuba, is a small stringed instrument somewhere between a guitar and an ukelele. It was created in Teguise where it is still made. The *timple* forms the background to two local folk dances: the *isa*, a jolly, country dance, and the *folia*, a more dignified, dance. Exhibits of traditional Canarian music and dance, or *verbena*, are held regularly throughout the islands.

Crafts

The wide variety of woods which grow on most of the islands has been the basis for much of Canary craftsmanship. Furniture, cedar chests and weaving looms are prime examples of the islanders' skills. **Basketwork** made from *cana* (cane) make ideal souvenirs.

Most of the islands' craftwork is extremely practical, and can be very decorative. *Vara* (twigwork), made from strips of chestnut, can be very attractive. *Palanqueta* work, made from date stems, is also a popular island craft. Crafts to look out for include the islands' unique **glazed pottery**, a legacy of the ancient Canarians, *traperas* (rag rugs), silk woven cloths, hand-embroidered *bordados* (tablecloths), costumed rag dolls, woollen shawls and polished green volcanic stone jewellery. Musical instruments like **castanets** (*chacaras*) and the local stringed *timple* make interesting gifts.

The most attractive Canarian craft souvenirs are the beautiful openwork or **embroidery**. The delicacy of the workmanship which local women put into producing this cloth is incredible – the most exquisite embroidery comes from Tenerife and La Palma.

Above: *Olive oil was once stored in clay jars like these, now used as decorative planters.*
Below: *Beautifully hand-embroidered tablecloths make excellent souvenirs.*

A DYING BUG

In 1825, agronomists introduced an industry to the Canary Islands, based around a tiny insect, *Dactylopius coccus*, which lives exclusively on a variety of cacti, from which cochineal is extracted by crushing the bugs. Cochineal, a crimson dye, earned the islanders a brief respite from economic decline, when it became the Canary Islands' most valuable export. Today, only a few farmers produce the dye, which involves the fastidious picking of the insects from prickly cactus leaves.

2
Las Palmas

More than just the capital of the eastern Canary Islands, Las Palmas today is a sprawling, cosmopolitan, multi-racial metropolis, similar to many large ports around the world but with a vibrancy and charm all of its own. Its population has doubled during the past 30 years to over 355,000 inhabitants and more than half of the Canarios now live here.

It's easy to see why. There's a wealth of interesting **museums** covering everything from Cro-Magnon man to Columbus, and several delightful churches. One of the top sights is the **Pueblo de Canario** in Doramas Park, an idealized Canarian village that presents a microcosm of the way island life used to be, complete with exuberant folk-dancing displays.

Early visitors included Phoenicians, Carthaginians and Moors, but it wasn't until the Spanish arrived in 1478 that the foundations of Las Palmas were laid. Stroll around the city's historic **Vegueta Quarter** to see the stamp of Spanish colonialism, from the narrow streets to ornate old buildings such as the beautiful **Casa de Colón** (Columbus's House).

Once you've had your fill of sightseeing, you can indulge in a little duty-free **shopping** in one of the many department stores, browse around the lively markets or head for the **beach** and relax on the wonderful golden sands of **Playa de las Canteras**. At the end of the day there are also numerous excellent restaurants and lively, atmospheric bars to keep you entertained for hours.

Don't Miss

*** Cathedral of Santa Ana: a wonderful mixture of Gothic, Baroque and neo-classical styles.
*** Santa Ana Plaza: Vegueta's busy main square.
*** Columbus's House: ornate façade with beautiful Renaissance interior.
*** Doramas Park: fascinating Canarian Village Museum filled with interesting ancient Canarian artefacts.

Opposite: *The cosmopolitan resort and commercial centre of Las Palmas, a city with a fascinating history.*

VEGUETA QUARTER

A tour of Las Palmas starts to the south of the port area in the historic Vegueta Quarter of the city. The oldest and most interesting sites are to be found here and it's a delightful place to wander around.

Plaza Santa Ana ★★★

Several bronze statues of the legendary giant Canary Island hound guard the entrance to the Plaza Santa Ana, Vegueta's main square. The dog is a symbol which has appeared on the Las Palmas coat-of-arms since 1506, and the island is supposed to have been named after it.

Santa Ana Cathedral ★★★

Plaza Santa Ana is dominated by the cathedral. Building began in 1497 but was constantly interrupted over the centuries, which is reflected in the cathedral's mixture of Gothic, Baroque and neo-Classical styles.

A treasure-house of relics, the cathedral's most precious artefact is the late 15th-century **Banner of the Conquest**, said to have been embroidered by Isabella I. Other works of art include a beautiful 1641 illuminated songbook, Felipe II's gold chalice, and Bishop Verdugo's pectoral cross and his throne, wrought by the 18th-century goldsmith, José Eugenio.

Diocesan Museum of Sacred Arts ★

This museum is housed in the cathedral and has a wonderful collection of **Aztec** and pre-Columbian treasures, rare paintings and tapestries as well as religious artefacts and sculptures. Open 09:00–14:00, 16:00–18:00 Mon–Fri, 09:00–14:00 Sat. Closed on Sunday.

FEATURES OF THE CASA DE COLON

The rooms of the Casa de Colón (Columbus's House) are large and airy, with high ceilings, small windows and huge doors. The interior design is spectacularly ornate, with impressive hardwood ceilings, great cedar beams, carved embellishments and finely panelled doors. As in this case, many early colonial buildings were also constructed with a large gateway, with huge, heavy doors, through which the occupier could drive his carriage directly into the courtyard. This gave access to an integral carriage-house built into the main structure. Often these large doors were not conventionally hinged, instead suspended on a peg-and-eye device made from iron.

Below: *The boat-filled marina at Las Palmas. The city is still a vital seaport.*

Above: *Casa de Colón, a superb example of early Renaissance Canarian architecture.*

'FLAMENCO' ART

The many churches of Gran Canaria and the four western islands contain some superb examples of ancient religious artistry, carvings, tapestries and statuary. Almost all of these treasures, dating from the 16th–17th centuries, were carved, painted, or woven by the great Flemish masters of Gothic ecclesiastical art. The reason for the proliferation of religious artworks in the five islands was that these islands were the producers of sugar and molasses, among the most expensive commodities in Europe at that time.

So, when sugar and its by-products were shipped to the Low Countries, the Flemish master craftsmen exchanged their religious artistry for the coveted cargoes.

In the **Plaza Santa Ana** there are also a number of other buildings of historic interest: the **Bishop's Palace**, the **Herreria**, **Casa de Los Hildagos** (the House of the Nobles) and the **Regent's House**. Palms line each side of the square, and the Colonial-style **Town Hall** (*ayuntamiento*), facing the cathedral, flies three flags: of Spain, Las Palmas and the flag of the Canaries. During the **Corpus Christi festival**, the square is beautifully decorated with a fantastic carpet of flowers.

Canarian Museum ★★

To the south of Plaza Santa Ana on Calle Dr Verneau is the Canarian Museum. The most important exhibits are those dealing with the ancient Canarians. There are Cro-Magnon skulls and fascinating examples of mummified Guanches, ceramics, tools, and weapons. A huge library of books dates back to the 15th century. The natural history and botanical section is also well worth a look. Open 10:00–17:00 Monday–Friday; 10:00–13:00 Saturday and 10:00–14:00 Sunday, tel: (928) 31 56 00. Closed on holidays.

Casa de Colón ★★★

Head towards the sea from the rear of the cathedral and turn into a narrow street-cum-square to find one of the best examples of early Canarian architecture. Although named Columbus's House (Casa de Colón), it is highly unlikely that Columbus actually lived here – he probably just visited for a few days in 1492. This mansion, with its ornate façade and beautiful Renaissance interior, dates from the end of the 15th century and was the home of the first Canarian governor. Today it has an interesting museum which recreates the Age of Discovery, complete with navigational aids, models and maps. The Casa de Colón also houses the **Provincial Archives** and **Fine Arts Museum**, with a portrait of Christopher Columbus as well as interesting works by Baroque artists Veronese, Divino Morales and Guido Reni. Some artwork has been donated by the **Prado Museum** in Madrid. Open 09:30–17:30 Monday–Friday and 09:30–13:00 on Saturday, closed Sunday and holidays, tel: (928) 31 12 55.

Hermitage of San Antonio Abad **

Just across the small, cobbled square from the Casa de Colón is the delightful, creeper-draped church where Columbus is thought to have prayed before setting off. The existing building dates mainly from 1796, and was restored in 1892 in order to commemorate Columbus's voyage 400 years before.

TRIANA DISTRICT

A dual carriageway separates the Vegueta Quarter from the city proper. Directly across the busy motorway from the Antonio Abad Square or Plaza is the main shopping thoroughfare of the Triana district of the city, the Calle Mayor de Triana, a predominantly pedestrianized zone with a wealth of gorgeous Art Nouveau buildings.

Plaza de Colón *

West of the Calle Mayor de Triana is the pretty Plaza de Colón, dominated by the **Church of San Francisco** and a fine statue of Columbus. To the south of this square are two more monuments to local heroes.

Pérez Galdós Theatre **

In the eastern corner of Triana district, between the promenade and Triana Street, is the Pérez Galdós Theatre, built in 1919. Home to the theatre and opera, this impressive Modernist building is named after the local novelist, **Benito Pérez Galdós**. There are murals by Néstor de la Torre in the foyer. Galdós's house, which is now a museum, is in Calle Caño nearby.

San Telmo Church *

Continuing east on Triana Street, by the Parque San Telmo, is the San Telmo Church which dates back to the 15th century. There's also a delightfully decorated **Art Nouveau** coffee kiosk, as well as the old army building from where General Franco announced his coup d'état on 18 July 1936. The main bus station is nearby, on the seaward side of the Avenida Maritima.

THE ARTS IN LAS PALMAS

The Pérez Galdós Theatre, sponsored by the island's *cabildo* (council), is host to the annual Festival of Opera from February to the middle of March. **The Spring Festival of Music and Dance** is also held here from April to May. These events are attended by top performers from around the world. The Gran Canaria Philharmonic Orchestra performs in the theatre regularly, as does the Las Palmas Philharmonic Orchestra.

Below: *A stunning Art Nouveau coffee kiosk adorns the corner of the Parque San Telmo.*

Above: *Folk-dancing display at the Canarian Village, an idealized version of a traditional pueblo in Doramas Park.*

Doramas Park ★★★

The Calle Mayor de Triana leads into the Calle Léon y Castillo. A few hundred metres further along is the beautiful Doramas Park, named after the last local Guanche chief.

The centrepiece of Doramas Park is the **Pueblo Canario**, a model island village that presents a rather romanticized view of Canarian society. The village was built in 1939 and was designed by the Canarian painter, **Néstor de la Torre**. This charming Canarian village has a museum that features many of De la Torre's best paintings. The museum is frequently used to stage traditional dance and music presentations. There are dancing displays on Thursday evenings. Open 10:00–13:00 Monday–Friday, 09:30–13:00 Saturday.

Further towards the port area of La Luz is the **Garden City** district, so-called because of the number of tree-lined avenues and streets dividing the residential area. Beyond the Garden City, fronting the **Alcaravanares** district, is the large **Nautical Club**, yacht basin and Naval Headquarters.

Santa Catalina ★

The next district north is the Santa Catalina area, heralded by the Santa Catalina Square. Here is the city centre proper. The **Tourist Office**, souvenir and craft market are located on the square. Duty-free shops cram the streets of Santa Catalina. There is a thriving open-air market on Sundays in the Santa Catalina Quarter of the city, called the **Mercado del Puerto**, facing the port area.

PUERTO DE LA LUZ

Named the 'Port of the Light' after the 16th-century fortress, the **Castillo de la Luz**, standing opposite one of the port's five piers, the **Muelle Pesquero**, is Europe's largest dock.

Because of its importance to Atlantic trade, this has become one of the world's most significant harbours. The present port was constructed in the late 19th century and expanded into the vast commercial area that it is now during the 20th century. The island's large fishing fleet is also based in this port.

Playa de la Canteras **

To the west of this narrow, peninsula-shaped neck of land is the beach of Las Palmas, Playa de la Canteras. Four kilometres (2½ miles) of fine white sand fronts the promenade, which is a typical town beach resort with bistros, hotels, nightclubs and even English-style pubs. The **Castillo de la Luz** fortress at the port's entrance in the La Isleta suburb is also worth a visit. Built in 1494 to repel pirate attacks, it is now home to an art gallery.

LAS PALMAS SHOPPING

Gran Canaria, and particularly Las Palmas, is a fun shopping area, not only for the selection of goods available, but more significantly, for the lack of import taxes, Spanish tax and the duty-free status of the island. The port area is always good for bargains, as are the shops along Calle Mayor de Triana and Calle Mesa y Lopez. Visit the **El Corte Inglés** department store, which is open all day and is stocked full of goods, or the **Galerías Preciados** for real bargains. They are both in Triana.

Municipal Market *

The Municipal Market (Mercado Central), in the Vegueta Quarter, is a must for lovers of the bustle of stall life and bargaining for traditional fare. Fresh and cured fish; fresh, cooked and preserved meats; cheeses from all over the islands; flowers; vegetables; herbs; spices; fruit and other local goods are rather temptingly displayed here.

Santa Catalina Park **

Usually a mass of colourful stalls, Santa Catalina Park bustles with life, where everything from leatherwork to postcards can be bought. You may even find a real bargain.

> **EL RASTRO**
>
> Visit **Santa Catalina Park**, in the centre of town, on Sunday morning. The entire plaza becomes a fascinating flea market, the **Rastro**, with more than 250 stalls. The market opens at roughly 09:00 and closes at 14:30. All around the square are cafés and bistros where you can relax and decide which stalls to visit before joining the melee. Everything from tacky souvenirs to leather goods, ceramics, craftwork, flowers and plants, second-hand items, antiques and books are hawked here. A variety of snacks, tapas and refreshments are on hand, and after a morning's browsing and buying, you can take a horse-drawn taxi carriage (*tartana*) to your favourite restaurant or back to the hotel.

Below: *Triana, a shopper's paradise for duty-free goods at bargain prices.*

Las Palmas at a Glance

The Canary Islands are ideal all year round for the sunny weather they always seem to offer. From the end of **October** to the end of **April** is generally considered the High Season. Many of the tourists from Europe book in advance for the months from **November** to **February** and note that the Christmas period is especially popular.

Most visitors from abroad, apart from those from the Spanish mainland, arrive by air at **Gando International Airport**, halfway between the capital and the south coast resorts. There are **ferry services** from Cádiz in Spain to Las Palmas for both passengers and cars. Arrange these sort of transfers when you are booking your accommodation.

Apart from taking organized **coach tours**, taking local **bus services**, or private **taxi** excursions in the island, the **hire-car** system is probably the best way to see this island's sights. If you bring your own car, however, you must bear in mind the following stipulations: you must have a valid driving licence, an International Driving Permit, a Green Card Insurance, a Vehicle Registration Document, a Bail Bond, a spare set of light bulbs, a red triangle warning sign, a change of headlights system and, of course, your passport. Main roads throughout the entire archipelago are excellent.

Hotels and accommodation in Las Palmas is varied as in most major cities around the world. Most hotels offer the usual facilities, some without a swimmimg pool and extra luxuries, like the **Parque Hotel**, located in the old city area, the **Rosalina**, a 3-star hotel between Catalina Park and the beach, and the **Iberia Sol Hotel**, not on the beach, but with excellent sea aspects. Apart from the beach-side hotels, the plusher hotels offering all ameneties, including a pool, are the **Santa Catalina** (host to the British and Spanish Royal families), **Mélia Cristina**, **Reina Isabel**, the **Concorde**, and **Sol Inn Bardinos**, the city's tallest hotel. A variety of apartment blocks are also available.

LUXURY

Melia Cristiana, Calle Gomera 6; tel: (928) 36 64 54, fax: 26 84 11; designed for high-spending businessmen.
Reina Isabel, Calle Alfredo L Jones 40; tel: (928) 26 01 00, fax: 27 45 58; close to Canteras Beach.
Santa Catalina, Parque Doramas, Calle Léon y Castillo 277; tel: (928) 24 30 40, fax: 24 27 64; in Doramas Park.

MID-RANGE

Sol Inn Bardinos, Calle Eduardo Benot 3; tel: (928) 26 61 00, fax: 22 91 39; a short walk from Catalina Park, Canteas beach and the port.
Concorde, Tomas Miller 85; tel: (928) 26 27 50, fax: 26 57 74; centrally located in the Santa Catalina district.
Melia Confort Iberia, Maritime Avenue-North; tel: (928) 36 11 33, fax: 36 13 44; on the seafront, not far from Alcaravaneras beach and the Nautical Club.
Imperial Playa, Calle Ferreras 1; tel: (928) 26 48 54, fax: 46 94 42; wide range of facilities, situated on Canteras beach.

BUDGET

Atlanta, Calle Alfredo L Jones 37; tel: (928) 22 26 71, fax: 27 34 85; located on Canteras beach with basic facilities.
Bajamar, Calle Venezuela 34; tel: (928) 27 62 54, fax: 27 62 54; Hotel apartments located a short distance from Paseo and main beach.
Gran Canaria, Paseo de Las Canteras; tel: (928) 27 50 78, fax: 26 24 20; fine location on Canteras beach with good facilities.
Parque, Muelle de Las Palmas 2; tel: (928) 36 80 00; efficient, business-like, situated between the old and new districts.
Olympia, Dr Grau Bassas 1, DP 35007; tel: (928) 26 17 20, fax: 26 26 17; centrally located and near bus transport.

Las Palmas at a Glance

WHERE TO EAT

Las Palmas is renowned for its incredible variety of eating places, from a mock steamboat, **The Mississippi**, moored in the Sporting Marina, to the eighth-floor luxury restaurant in the **Hotel Reina Isabel**. There are also Japanese and **Chinese**, **Russian** or Lebanese restaurants, **tapas bars** and **bistros**. There are several vegetarian restaurants in the city, and even one serving typically British fare. For succulent food the following come highly recommended:

El Novillo Precoz, Calle Portugal 9; tel: (928) 22 16 59; behind Playas Canteras with Argentinian-style meat dishes. **Casa Julio**, Calle Naval 123; tel: (928) 46 01 39; Canarian and fish dishes located in port sector. Closed Sunday.
Pasta Real, Calle Secretario Padilla 28; tel: (928) 26 22 67; not strictly Canarian, but this is where to find some of the city's best pasta and delicious vegetarian dishes.

SHOPPING

Las Palmas is a mecca for shoppers with goods at duty-free prices. August is best for the sales and prices of watches, cameras, electrical goods, perfumes, wines, tobacco etc. are often lower than in resort shops. The port area and both **Calle Mayor de Lopez** are good for bargains. The **El**

Corte Ingles store is open all day and the **Glaerias Preciados** are worth a visit. The Municipal Market, or **Mercado Central**, in Vegueta Quarter, is a bustle of stall life with bargaining for traditional fare. Fresh and cured fish, fresh, cooked and preserved meats, cheeses from the islands, flowers, vegetables, herbs, spices, fruit and other local goods are displayed here. There is a thriving open-air market on Sundays in the Santa Catalina Quarter called the **Mercado del Puerto**, facing the port. Santa Catalina Park is a mass of colourful stalls selling local souvenirs, ranging from leatherwork to needlework and postcards. Open 09:00–13:00, 16:00–20:00 Monday–Friday. In the summer months, many shops stay open all morning from 08:00–14:00 and often late into the night on festival and holidays.

TOURS AND EXCURSIONS

Tourist buses and some taxi companies offer a variety of tours. The Tourist Office on Catalina Park has leaflets on tours both in the city and to the island's interior.

Tours include the Vegueta quarter; main shopping areas; the Canario Museum, the Canarian Village in Doramas Park and the nearby Néstor Museum. There are many options, both day and night, from the **Grand Tour** of the interior and the **Jeep Safari** to the mountains, to the **Scala Cabaret** and **Casino** night, or the Wild West night at **Sioux City**. You can also take a trip to **Morocco** in North Africa for a day's sightseeing and shopping.

USEFUL CONTACTS

Tourist Board, Parque Santa Catalina, Las Palmas; tel: (928) 26 46 23 or (928) 27 16 00.
Patronado de Turismo, Léon y Castillo 17, Las Palmas; tel: (928) 36 24 22 / 36 26 22. Fax: (928) 36 28 22.
Council of Tourism and Transport, Plaza de los Detechos Humanos, s/n Edificio Usos Multiples, 6th and 7th Floors, 35003 Las Palmas; tel: (928) 36 16 00/ 36 11 56. fax: (928) 38 06 16.
Aeropuerto de Gando, tel: (928) 25 41 40.
IBERIA Airlines, Avenida Ramirez Béthancourt, Las Palmas; tel: (928) 37 02 22.

EAST CANARY ISLANDS	J	F	M	A	M	J	J	A	S	O	N	D
AVERAGE TEMP. °C	16	17	17	18	19	20	23	23	21	21	18	17
AVERAGE TEMP. °F	61	63	63	64	66	68	73	73	70	70	64	63
HOURS OF SUN DAILY	7	7	8	8	9	9	10	8	8	8	7	6
DAYS OF RAINFALL	7	6	5	4	2	1	1	1	2	6	10	9
RAINFALL mm	36	8	2	11	2	-	-	-	6	3	58	9
RAINFALL in	1.5	0	0	0.5	0	0	0	0	0	0	2	0

3
Gran Canaria

Lying almost at the heart of the Canary archipelago, Gran Canaria is a fascinating island: an exhilarating blend of old and new. Most visitors head for its superb sandy beaches, attracted by the year-round sun, superb watersports and hectic nightlife. The capital, **Las Palmas**, is another big draw; a sophisticated, cosmopolitan city packed with beautiful old buildings and excellent for shopping.

Yet beyond the beaches lies an eye-catching natural wonderland virtually unscathed by modern development and preserving centuries-old culture within its domain. Gran Canaria is known as a 'continent in miniature' because of its tremendously varied terrain. Arid deserts, rugged mountains and rocky gorges contrast with lush tropical forests, banana plantations, vineyards and sugar canes. Scattered throughout the interior are charming whitewashed villages and ancient archaeological sites, relics of the long vanished Guanche civilization.

Gando International Airport is situated on the east coast, almost midway between Las Palmas to the north and the **Maspalomas** resort on the southeast coast. An excellent motorway runs down the east side of the island and a secondary road circumnavigates Gran Canaria, with winding routes linking the picturesque towns and villages in the interior. Whether you wish to soak up the sun, shop till you drop, explore the island's breathtaking scenery or discover its historic past, Gran Canaria is the perfect place for a wonderful holiday.

DON'T MISS

*** **Telde:** original capital, nearby Cuatro Puertas, ancient Guanche site.
*** **Teror:** 16th-century basilica and sanctuary of the Virgin of the Pines.
*** **Aldea Valley** and **Aldea Mirador:** spectacular east coast views.
*** **Gáldar:** historic site, fascinating painted cave with Guanche pictographs.
** **Ingenio:** oldest village on island, lace-making centre and Stone Museum.

Opposite: *The lovely, sheltered beach of Puerto Rico, excellent for watersports.*

Gran Canaria

THE COASTAL RESORTS

Apart from the 4km-long (2½ mile) **Canteras Beach** to the west of Las Palmas, there are three other major resorts on the southern coast of the island, which could almost be called the Costa Canaria since it has so much in common with the costas on the Spanish mainland. The resorts are places you'll either love or hate. Both **Playa de Inglés** and **Maspalomas** attract the lion's share of tourists, who come for the usual sun and fun found in beach resorts all over the world. These two conurbations have more or less merged into one long mass of high and low-rise buildings fronting a vast sandy beach, which has excellent water-sport facilities. Maspalomas also boasts **Holiday World** – a large amusement park complete with ferris wheel, dodgems and laser games. Not far west of Maspalomas is the third resort of **Puerto Rico**. South of Maspalomas is a great expanse of sand dunes which resemble a mini-Sahara, with a long, undeveloped beach running around a large headland, protected from development.

Above: *The natural beauty of the sand dunes in Maspalomas is quite outstanding.*

Other popular resorts along the south coast include **San Agustín**, **Arguineguín** and **Puerto del Mogán**. Many resorts are high-rise, concrete sprawls but they all have superb facilities. **Puerto del Mogán** is a lovely place, with picturesque whitewashed villas and a very smart marina. There's a string of excellent sandy beaches around the island and those on the east coast are much quieter.

A COASTAL TOUR

It is possible to tour around the island's coast, 245km (152 miles) long, in a full day – but you'll have to start rather early. If you take the main road south out of Las Palmas, and travel past Vegueta and the Castillo San Cristóbal, the turning for Telde will be visible. This road will take you into the town.

Telde ★★★

This is the second largest town on the island, apart from the tourist conurbations. The first colonial settlement, Telde was originally the seat of the last Guanche king, **Doramas**, and it is now divided into three districts. **San Juan** district is named after the 15th-century volcanic rock-built Church of St John the Baptist, which contains a magnificent, 500-year-old gilt-wood Flemish altarpiece, a 16th-century image of Christ created from maize cobs donated by the Tabasco Indians of Mexico, and a

Above: *Boats and water-front at the picturesque resort of Puerto de Mogán.*

wonderful painting by the well-known Italian artist Vicenzo Carducci. The **San Francisco** district is named after the Convent of San Francisco, which is well known for its elaborate interior panelling. **Los Llanos** district was originally the peasant quarter, home to the Moorish and black slaves who once worked the island's sugar plantations.

Keeping on the same road, the Guanche mausoleum of **Cuatro Puertas** (the Four-Doored Mountain), can be visited just off the road to the left. Today the cave burial sites have been turned into goat pens.

Ingenio ★★

This was a town which was founded by the Portuguese and it has inherited a tradition of witchcraft and superstition from the large slave population which inhabited the area for a long time. Stop briefly at **Museo de Piedras e Artesania Canaria**, to see the interesting Guanche artifacts and the fascinating display of old farm tools and rocks at Ingenio which is also famous for its fine embroidery work.

If you rejoin the main road south, you'll see that the Aeroclub is indicated to the left and a short detour right will take you up into the picturesque Barranco Berriel, to the dramatic scenery of the **Aguila Canyon**. Back on the road, by-pass Playa de Inglés and Maspalomas, where you will join the beautiful coastal route with views of fine bays from **Pasito Blanco**, through to the resort area of Puerto Rico, to just before Playa de Mogán, where the steep-sided **Barranco de Mogán** channels the road inland.

A KING'S LAST STAND

In the extreme northwest corner of Gran Canaria is a weird rock formation riddled with gaunt caverns. Near the town of **Gáldar**, this site was once the centre of the realm of **Tenesor Semidan**, the Guanche king. In 1483 he was beaten by the Spanish and forcibly converted to Christianity by being baptized here. After his conversion he made peace with the Spanish and persuaded his followers to do the same.

Valley of La Aldea ★★★

The road from Mogán follows the panoramic Valley of La Aldea to a lookout, the **Mirador de Balcon** – a photographer's dream. The next stop, **El Risco**, has a pretty little beach. Frightening switchbacks pass two roadside crosses and a number of lookout sites. Stop at the **Dedo de Díos**, Finger of God mirador, just before Agaete town. Below here is the **Puerto de Las Nieves**, a banana shipping port and fishing village. Be adventurous and try one of the excellent restaurants here for a meal of locally caught, freshly prepared fish.

After lunch, pay a visit to **Agaete** to see the Hermitage of La Virgen de Las Nieves with its fine 16th-century Flemish triptych (painted panel) of the Madonna and Child. This region is perfect for cultivating fruit and vegetables. Between Agaete and Gáldar at the next stop are two sites on the right of the road: Cave of the Crosses and the Hermitage of Saint Isidro de Viejo.

Gáldar ★★★

The town of Gáldar was home to the last local chief, **Tenesor Semidan**, and has several interesting historic sites, including the ancient **Painted Cave** (Cueva Pintada), with wonderful examples of colourful, geometric Guanche designs and the **Tumulo de la Guancha**, an ancient cemetery. The Town Hall, fronted by a magnificent dragon tree, has a museum of Guanche artefacts. The 18th-century church, built on the site of Tenesor Semidan's palace, contains a 15th-century green ceramic font thought to come from Andalucia and to have been used in the forcible conversion of the indigenous inhabitants during the Spanish conquest.

After Gáldar, the road strides out over the Vega Mayor plain, from **Santa María de Guia**. This pretty village is known for its tasty goat's milk and delicious thistle-flower cheese. It also has a lovely, tiny church, with wonderful sculptures by José Lujan Pérez, who was born at nearby Tres Palmas. This quaint little village also has a connection with the French composer, Camille Saint-Saëns, who lived in Llanos de Parra, just up the road.

RAINMAKERS OF RAMA

Literally, one of the most striking festivals of the Canaries occurs during summer in Agaete, on the northwest coast of Gran Canaria. This is the festival of the Rama. So popular is the ritual that locals vary the date to keep the number of attendees down. Dating back to Guanche days, the fiesta involves locals congregating in the mountains above the town and marching to the coast armed with green boughs. Upon reaching the sea, they beat the water with branches, in the age-old ritual of invoking rain from the Gods. The procession culminates in a heaving sea of bodies celebrating Rama with music and dancing in the streets of Agaete.

Arucas **

This historic town was originally the site of the
Hermitage of San Pedro, when Pedro Perón, the island's
governor, established it in 1526. Apart from a superb
Municipal Park, the town's main claim to fame is its
early 20th-century parish church, built in neo-Gothic
style, and resembling a city cathedral.

Up on a hill here, a botanical garden and mirador has
been laid out for views over the fertile valley and plain.

Teror ***

Instead of returning to Las Palmas via the coastal road,
take a detour into the mountains up to the elegant town of
Teror. It is a small, northern town with lovely wide streets
lined with colonial houses. It was here, in 1481, that the
Madonna was said to have appeared in a pine tree, estab-
lishing the town as a centre of pilgrimage. Notable sites in
the town include the 18th-century, neo-Classical-style
Nuestra Señora del Pino basilica and jewelled shrine, the
18th-century neo-Gothic tower and the Bishop's Palace.

A MOUNTAIN TOUR

This could be either a day or half-day tour, depending on
the time spent at each site. This tour takes the visitor
across the crown of the island, where you will see five
important inland sites.

Below: *Gran Canaria's
maritime importance was
underpinned by superb
natural harbours, which
today cater more for
pleasure boats than
commercial vessels.*

Viera y Clavijo
Jardín Canario ***

Take the road out of
Las Palmas along the
motorway between
the Vegueta and
Triana districts. The
road leads up to the
Viera y Clavijo Jardín
Canario, a spectacu-
lar botanical garden.
This garden has a
magnificent collection

HONEYCOMB HILL

In northwest Gran Canaria a volcanic mass known as the **Cuesta de Silva** stands near Santa María de Guía. One mountain face, called the **Cenobio de Valerón**, is a great arc of stone, overhung by a steep ledge. High up, and apparently inaccessible, numerous small caves have been carved out of the cliff face by the Guanches. Modern steps now lead up to the caverns. Wooden doors once covered the caves' entrances, and historians dispute as to whether they were utilized as grain silos, or if they were pre-marital refuges for eligible native maidens.

of flora on show including the dragon trees and cactus garden. Continue up through the narrow part of Tafira and follow the signs to the golf course perched on top of the volcanic crater of the same name.

Santa Brígida ★★
Returning to the main road, the next stop is Santa Brígida town. Once known as Sataute, or Little Palm Tree, this typical Canarian agricultural town, surrounded by palms, stands on the brink of a ravine. The church contains a lovely sculpture of Christ by a local artist. The town is also famous for its wonderful pottery work.

Vega de San Mateo ★
If you do this tour on a Saturday or Sunday, don't miss the fruit and flower market in the next village, Vega de San Mateo. The local markets are open in the mornings. Take a walk around it to see what the people like to eat.

Cross of Tejeda ★★
From here, the road winds up, with two fine miradors on the right hand side, to the summit of the main route, the Cruz, or Cross of Tejeda at 1450m (4757ft). A National Parador hotel is located here.

Above: *Villages sheltered by mountains are a typical sight in the rugged interior.*
Below: *The Cruz de Tejeda, a popular vantage point overlooking magnificent natural scenery.*

Above: *Spectacular panoramas abound in the interior. Here, pine forests are backed by Roque Nubio.*

Roque Nubio ★★

The spectacular pinnacle of the Roque Nubio (Cloud Rock), 1817m (5961ft) high, rises magnificently from the bleak volcanic landscape. Look out for the huge boulders named **El Fraile** (The Monk) and **Roque Bentaiga**. In the distance, you will be able to see the outline of the spectacular Teide mountain on nearby Tenerife, to the west. From the road here, take the side route up to the island's peak, the 1949m-high (6394ft) **Pico de las Nieves**, for breathtaking views.

Artenara ★★

Back at Tejeda Parador, make another detour to the west. This side road leads around the peak of **Moriscos**, at 1771m (5810ft), to the isolated village of Artenara, nestled in countryside surrounded by cave-riddled gorges and cross-crowned peaks. The main attaction here is the small hermitage known as the **Cueva de la Virgen**, a shrine cut out of the volcanic rock.

There is a fine panoramic view from the **Mirador la Silla** here, and in the distance, to the northwest, is the peak of Tamadaba Mountain, 1444m (4738ft) high and surrounded by the forests of the Pinar de Tamadaba. Returning to the Parador, it will probably be time for lunch, which you should have before setting off on the spectacular drive through the island's highest mountains. Leave room for a dessert so that you can sample some of the island's finest in the next village.

The road south from the Parador leads through the village of **Tejeda**, renowned for its delicious cakes. The route now winds precariously around the Cloud Rock to the right, and across the Barranco de Ayacate, with breathtaking views of the **Pico de las Nieves** to the left.

TROGLODYTES

Just northwest of Tejeda is one of the most charming villages on Gran Canaria, **Artenara**. Most of its dwellings are carved out of the precipitous volcanic rock. Set in pine forests, Artenara is built into the mountainside and is the island's highest village. Even the church, **La Virgen de la Cuevita** (of the Little Cave), melts into the rockface, surmounted by a tiny bell tower. Look for door number nine. This will lead you through the mountainside to a ledge which has been transformed into a cliff-side restaurant.

San Bartolomé de Tirajana ★★★

Just before entering the town of San Bartolomé de Tirajana, the landscape is dotted with caves, notably those of **Del Pinar** and the **Cuevas Blancas**. Known in Guanche times as Tamaran, San Bartolomé de Tirajana is built in the vast crater of Tirajana, under the shadow of the central massif of the island. The final vestiges of Guanche were routed here by the conquistador **Pedro de Vera**, who laid siege to the last natives until they starved. The surrealistic landscape here is covered with trees, orchards and almond groves interspersed with pine, cherry and plum trees mixed with palms. This is the most visited attraction in the entire Canaries, and the views from the **Mirador Posador** are certainly exceptional. The Posador is a small hotel which bakes its own bread in an ancient traditional oven. From here a road leads directly south, through the marvellously picturesque **Fataga Ravine**, down to the coast at Maspalomas.

Santa Lucía ★★

From San Bartolomé you can either take the Fataga road, or head for the east coast along the main road which runs through **Santa Lucía** village. Apart from Santa Lucía's delightful white-washed church, the village has an ethnological museum which, as well as exhibiting many fascinating artifacts of Guanche life and death, and a collection of mummies, also houses a typical 17th-century Canarian room. The **Museum La Fortaleza**, contained in a mock fort, also has a restaurant, and Guanche artefacts provide an atmospheric backdrop to a typically Canarian meal. There are some artisan shops in Santa Lucía which are worth visiting.

Temisas ★

As the road leaves Santa Lucía, the **Fortaleza Grande** is visible just off to the right. Temisas, to the left, is a renowned olive-producing area. Between here and the next village, the road is chiselled through the red rock, and some exciting Guanche remains have been excavated in the **Balos** and **Guayadeque** gorges near here.

BARRANCO VEGETATION

A *barranco* is a generally dried up riverbed, either founded by twisted lava beds, or carved out by the forces of nature into a steep sided gorge. There are several notable barrancos on Gran Canaria, often much greener than you'd expect. Apart from palms and pines, of which the endemic species is *Pinus canariensis*, look for the finger-like succulent, *Euphorbia canariensis*, the pink rock-rose, *Cistus symphytifolius*, and the primordial vegetation, Aeonium. The dwarf yellow broom, *Teline microphylla*, is prevalent, as are clumps of balos bushes.

Below: *Vintage transport still navigates the treacherous mountain roads.*

Gran Canaria at a Glance

BEST TIMES TO VISIT

Winter is the favourite time to visit Gran Canaria for most Europeans, although this is the busiest time of the year. British visitors arrive all year round as a suntan is almost guaranteed and the waters are warm enough to swim comfortably. The climate in the south of the island is generally better than that in the north.

GETTING THERE

Most visitors from abroad, except those from the Spanish mainland, arrive by air at **Gando International Airport**, just south of the capital. There are **ferry services** from Cádiz in Spain for passengers and cars to Las Palmas.

GETTING AROUND

Car hire is the most popular way of getting around the island. Apart from hiring a car and doing your own thing, there are an enormous number of **coach tours** which can be joined at hotels or pre-designated pick-up points. Should you bring your own **car** on the ferry, make sure you have the right documents, drive on the right and wear seat belts, which are compulsory.

WHERE TO STAY

Many visitors to the islands opt for **apartment accommodation**, and Gran Canaria has a huge choice of apartment blocks, not only in Las Palmas, but in the resort areas of Playa del Inglés, Bahia Feliz, Puerto Rico, Maspalomas, San Agustin and Arguineguin or Patalavaca.

Agaete
BUDGET
Princess Guayarmina, Los Berrazales; tel: (928) 89 80 09, fax: 89 85 25; basic facilities but with a swimming pool.

Arucas
MID-RANGE
Bella Arehucas, Calle Panchito Hernandez 10; tel: (928) 60 06 51; beautiful and convenient location for touring.

San Agustin
LUXURY
Melia Tamarindos, Calle Retamas 3; tel: (928) 77 40 90, fax: 77 40 91; superior facilities in excellent location.

MID-RANGE
Ifa Beach Hotel, Los Jazamines 25; tel: (928) 76 51 00, fax: 76 85 99; one of the best-priced accommodation options in this region with good pool.

BUDGET
Inter Club Atlantis, Los Jazamines 2; tel: (928) 76 09 50, fax: 76 09 74; reasonably priced, good facilities, pool.

San Bartolomé de Tirijana
LUXURY
Folias, Calle Las Retamas 17; tel: (928) 76 24 50; basic facilities but good location.

MID-RANGE
Beverly Park, Hamburgo 2 (Playa del Ingles); tel: (928) 76 17 50, fax: 76 18 12; good location; golf course and pool.

Playa del Inglés
LUXURY
Apolo, Avenida Estados Unidos 28; tel: (928) 76 00 58, fax: 76 3918; excellent range of facilities plus swimming pool.
Las Margeritas, Avenida Gran Canaria 38; tel: (928) 76 11 12, fax: 76 53 80; wide range of facilities and swimming pool.
Lucana, Plaza del Sol 1; tel: (928) 77 40 40, fax: 77 41 41; perfect location with good pool and wide range of facilities.

MID-RANGE
Rey Carlos, Avenida Tirijana 14; tel: (928) 76 01 16, fax: 76 29 45; good position, pool and range of services.
Continental, Avenida de Italia 2; tel: (928) 76 16 05, fax: 77 14 84; a medium-size hotel for this kind of resort, with a good pool.
Wakiki, Avenida de Gran Canaria 20; tel: (928) 76 23 00; good location and wide range of facilities for price, pool.

BUDGET
Ifa Regina Mar, Avenida EE. UU. 38; tel: (928) 76 76 16, fax: 76 51 67; good price for this fairly basic hotel, good pool.

Maspalomas
LUXURY
Iberotel Maspalomas Oasis, Playa de Maspalomas, tel: (928) 76 01 70, fax: 14 11 92; the top hotel on this resort, all facilities.

MID-RANGE
Ifa Faro, Playa de Maspalomas; tel: (928) 14 22 14, fax: 14 19 40;

Gran Canaria at a Glance

rather limited facilities and services, but good pool.
Palm Beach, Avenida del Oasis s/n; tel: (928) 76 29 20, fax: 14 18 08; a sophisticated hotel.

BUDGET
Green Golf Apartments, Campo de Golf; tel: (928) 77 39 49; facilities for children, 3 pools.
Riu Palace Meloneras, Playa de Maspalomas; tel: (928) 14 31 82; short walk from beach.

Puerto de Mogán
MID-RANGE
Guest House Silene, Tomas Zerolo 9; tel: (928) 33 01 99; convenient to local facilities, homely atmosphere.

Puerto Rico
LUXURY
Revoli, Avenida del Mogán; tel: (928) 56 12 58, fax: 56 20 96; best facilities in this resort.

MID-RANGE
Rio Sol, Cornisa 24; tel: (928) 74 51 48, fax: 56 07 74; apartments with pool.

WHERE TO EAT

San Agustin
San Agustín Beach Club, tel: (928) 76 04 00; seafood.
Chez Mario, Los Pinos, s/n, San Bartolome de Tirijana; tel: (928) 76 18 17; inexpensive Italian dishes, pleasant surroundings.

Playa del Inglés
Meson Viuda de Franco, Avda. Tirijana 2; tel: (928) 76 03 71; international specialities.

Bali, Avenida Bonn 23, tel: (928) 76 32 61; good Indonesian fare.

Also in the South
Las Cumbres, Avenida Tirijana 9; tel: (928) 76 09 41; varied international menu.
Casa del Abuelo, Calle Alfereces Provisionales 11; tel: (928) 76 44 11; local fare.

Tejeda
El Refugio, Cruz de Tejeda; tel: (928) 66 61 88; terrace service.

Arguineguin
Restaurant del Mar; harbour views, excellent fare.

Telde
Pablo Silva, Calle General de El Goro 1; tel: (928) 57 46 82; fine Canarian dishes.
La Pardilla, Calle Raimundo Lulio 54, tel: (928) 69 51 02; Canarian and International fare.

Tafira Alta
La Masia de Canarias, Calle Murillo 36; tel: (928) 35 01 20; excellent Canarian food.

TOURS AND EXCURSIONS

There are numerous options for organized or individual tours. Many independent **coach** companies offer various trips from one hour to full-day outings. Hotels display a selection of organized tours with guides, or an official **Tourist Board** can recommend a number of alternatives such as the North Africa Tour to Morocco. Several tour operators offer day-long

excursions which fly you to the village of El-Aaiun for its fascinating camel market, souks and typical Moroccan way of life.
Donkey or **camel safaris:** Safaris, Carretera de Faro de Maspalomas.
Deep-sea fishing: Club Nautico Metropole, Paseo Alonso Quesada; tel: (928) 24 43 46.
Flying, parachuting, sky-diving: Aeroclub Maspalomas, tel: (928) 76 24 47.
Golf: Campo de Golf de Maspalomas, Avenida de Africa; tel: (928) 76 25 81.
Sailing: Escuela Territorial de Vela de Puerto Rico, Calle Doreste, Puerto Rico; tel: (928) 56 07 72.
Watersports: Sun Club, Playa del Inglés; tel: (928) 76 09 50.
Casablanca, Marrakesh or **Agadir:** Guillermo Sintes Reyes SA. Calle Artemi Semidan 11, 3rd Floor, Las Palmas, tel: (928) 27 71 53, 27 72 08 or 27 41 14.

₀USEFUL CONTACTS

Tourist Board, Parque Santa Catalina, Las Palmas; tel: (928) 26 46 23 or 27 16 00.
Tourist Office, Playa del Inglés, Ave de España; tel: (928) 77 15 50
Patronado de Turismo, Léon y Castille 17, Las Palmas; tel: (928) 36 24 22, fax: 36 28 22.
Council of Tourism and Transport, Plaza de los Detechos Humanos, s/n Edificio Usos Multiples, 6th and 7th Floors, 35003 Las Palmas, tel: (928) 36 16 00/ 36 11 56. fax: (928) 38 06 16.

4
Fuerteventura

Fuerteventura is the largest of the Canary Islands after Tenerife and is arid and desert-like. It is known as the '**Viejo Pais Canario**', or the 'Old Country', as it echoes the conditions of its mother country, Africa, just 90km (56 miles) to the east. The countryside has been denuded by both man and goat, and, with little rainfall, the island is practically devoid of vegetation and has a tiny population. It is rather stark and bare but it does have some of the most glorious beaches – miles and miles of lovely, soft sand. It can get a bit windy at times but for the avid wind-surfer this is the ideal place to visit!

Terracing, windmills, and jealously guarded water collection pools enable the locals to wrest a meagre crop of maize, alfalfa, wheat, barley, chick peas, pineapples and a few vegetables from the cindery and sandy soil. The many goats and chickens provide meat, but some Fuerteventurans turn to the sea for its abundant harvest.

With the longest coastline of the Canary group, the island stretches over 100km (62 miles) in length. It is this beautiful coastline that attracts the visitors who select the island for its isolation, tranquility and perfect beaches. The island is divided into two – the bulbous, **northern** two-thirds, with its historic sites and national park of dunes and wildlife, and the long, narrow peninsula of **Jandía**, with its celebrated beach resorts, in the south. Inland, volcanic mountain ranges dot the landscape, traversed by dried-up riverbeds, which have cut ravines through the wide regions of the *malpaís*, the cinder-strewn 'badlands'.

Lanzarote
Arrecife

Puerto del
Rosario
Las Palmas   *Fuerteventura*
Gran
Canaria

<table>
<tr><td colspan="1">DON'T MISS</td></tr>
</table>

*** National Underwater Park: finest submarine park in the Canaries.
** Valley of Palms: oasis with ancient buildings.
** Pájara Parish Church: fine example of 16th-century architecture.
** Jandía Mountain: highest point on the island, magnificent views.
** La Oliva: 18th-century colonial buildings.
** Dunes National Park: mini-Sahara of undulating white sand dunes.

Opposite: *The windswept Jandía peninsula with 26km (16 miles) of glorious sandy beaches.*

Fuerteventura

Man-made Attractions

Apart from the numerous natural attractions of
Fuerteventura, the island also has a number of fascinating
architectural monuments. Jean de Béthancourt, the first
colonist, founded the **Santa María Cathedral** at Betancuria
as early as the first years of the 15th century, but it
was destroyed by pirates in 1539. The site, set in the wild
interior, is dramatic. Later, Franciscan monks built several
beautiful hermitages and churches throughout the island,

notably at **El Time**, **La Olivia**, **Antigua**, and **Pájara**. Most are well preserved and immensely photogenic, as are the island's many windmills. Some of the mills are still operational. One is now a restaurant, and others lend their picturesque silhouettes to the barren skyline. Colonists left several ancient forts behind, reminders of the Canary Islands' violent history. **El Tostón** castle, at Costillo, is a fine example of the island's early fortifications. Civil architecture from the past includes the grandiose **Casa de los Coroneles** at La Olivia, which dates back to the 18th century.

PUERTO DEL ROSARIO

The capital city of Fuerteventura has changed location several times over the past century or so. In 1836, the town of **Betancuria** took over the mantle of capital from **Antigua**, and, in 1860, the town of **Puerto de Cabras**, (Port of Goats), founded in 1797, became the island's administrative centre. In 1957, for a variety of reasons, the name of Cabras was changed to Puerto del Rosario (Port of the Rosary). The city is located on a natural bay on the eastern side of the island. The long harbour arm and portside installations were built as early as 1837. Today, the port supports a large fishing fleet and is home to the inter-island ferries.

Around the Town

The population of Puerto del Rosario is around 8500, excluding the Foreign Legion. The seat of Government is located here, as are the headquarters and barracks of the **Foreign Legion**. Below the Legionnaire's office, in beautiful, terraced gardens, there is a celebration of the exploits of the Legion in an interesting collection of statues, momentoes, memorials and weaponry.

Below: *Military statues reflect past glories in the gardens of the Spanish Foreign Legion's barracks.*

CORRALEJO

Pelayo
Pizarro C. Juan XXIII
Lallermand
Pérez Galdós
Fontán
J. de Austria
Lope
El Charco
Manuel Velázquez
Tomás de Aquino
Díaz Trayter
Almirante
Hispanidad
de Mayo
(H)
Jesús y María
La Cruz
J. de Béthancourt
León y Castillo
de los Reyes de España
García Escámez
Rosario
(H)
(i)
San Roque
León y Castillo
José Secundino Alonso
La Mancha
La Venta
Rocinante
Miño
Duero
Tajo
ANTIGUA
AIRPORT

ATLANTIC
OCEAN

N

0   500 m
0   500 yds

Puerto del Rosario

Puerto del Rosario is said to be the brain-child of a past mayor, who dictated that no building in the city should exceed a certain height, and even now only one skyscraper dominates the skyline. Although there aren't really old buildings here, the old part of the town, with its narrow cobbled streets and restful squares, is certainly worth exploring, as are the craft shops like **Artesania**.

Playa Blanca *

Many of the visitors avoid Rosario and head for the beaches, or the older and more interesting towns and sites on the island. In the first week of October, Puerto del Rosario holds its annual festival, the **Fiesta de la Virgen de Rosario**. Just south of the city is a beautiful beach, Playa Blanca, which is over-looked by the **National Parador**. Another kilometre further south is the island's only airport which lies between the coastal road and the sea.

NORTH FROM PUERTO DEL ROSARIO

The main road north, towards La Olivia, passes the old airport and Devil's Claw mountain before a track leads off to the left towards the **Las Mercedes Hermitage** at El Time village. Further along the main road, just before La Oliva Plain, there is a monument to the well-known exiled writer Miguel de Unamuno on **Montaña Quemada** or Burnt Mountain.

The fascinating town of **La Oliva** boasts the interesting 18th-century military residence **Casa de los Coroneles**, the Aztec-style fronted **Casa del Capellan**, and the 18th-century **Nuestra Señora de Candelaria**.

HOW DID FUERTEVENTURA GET ITS NAME?

Fuerteventura in ancient times was a lush, fertile island known as **Herbania**. Ecological disasters make this name inappropriate today. Conquistadore Jean de Béthancourt is supposed to have said 'Que fuerte ventura!' (what a great adventure) when he first landed. The name might be a corruption of *el viento fuerte* – the name for the strong wind which blows almost constantly.

Dramatic in its lonely surroundings, the Casa de los Coroneles dates from the 18th- century and was the residence of the military commanders of the island up until the end of the 19th century. The coat of arms over its entrance gate is surmounted by a cross and is indicative of Spain's Catholic influence. Its balconies are also typical of Canarian workmanship. Towers at each end of the façade give the building a fortified look.

Past La Oliva, a road west leads to **El Cotillo**, the 15th-century site of **Maxorata**, seat of **King Guixe** of the Guanches. Cotilla is a small fishing village and there are some lovely beaches nearby.

Heading towards **Puerto del Tostón** you will come across the well-known resort of **Caleta Fueste** and the tiny fishing port which is overlooked by the fascinating antique **Rico Roque** tower.

On the road towards **Corralejo**, take time to scale **Bayuyo Peak** for breathtaking scenic views. An easy climb to the summit affords vistas across volcanic cinders and sand dunes to the **Isle of Lobos** to the north, and the peak of **Caldera Hondo** (272m; 870ft) to the south.

LOCAL CUSTOMS

Like many European countries with a hot climate, the tradition of the *siesta* continues on most of the islands. Between 13:00 and 16:00 towns and villages will be eerily deserted, so this isn't a good time to go sightseeing or shopping. Locals will be enjoying a long lunch and a short nap, so why not do the same? The *paseo* (promenade) is the early evening stroll where families parade in their finery before going off to eat at 20:00.

Below: *The busy ferry terminal and popular resort of Corralejo.*

Above: *Corralejo's sparsely vegetated sand dunes, now a national park and habitat for rare birds.*

Corralejo **

This popular resort is situated on the northern tip of the island. The fishing port is flanked by rolling dunes giving way to fabulous sandy resort beaches. Corralejo is known throughout the Canary islands for its beaches, but its centre has been a little spoilt by modernization. Local fishermen, however, still congregate in bars by the quayside, and their gaily painted craft add colour to the small port. From here you can hop onto the ferry across **El Rio** to the nearby islet of **Lobos** (Wolf Island, named for its seals, or sea-wolves), or to the distant island of **Lanzarote**.

Both of the region's wonderful beaches, **Playa de Corralejo** and **Playa del Moro**, lie to the east of the town.

Dunes National Park **

The road east from the outskirts of the town passes the Corralejo Beach Hotel complex and follows the edge of the Dunes National Park as it hugs the coastline back to Puerto del Rosario. The park – a vast desert – is also a nature reserve for several species of rare birds, some of which breed here. Where there is any vegetation, mostly in the gullies and dry gorges to the edge of the sandy desert, the North African ground squirrel will be found among sparse glasswort, sea spurge and tamarisk.

Playa del Perchel *

As the road nears the city, the scenery gives way to small volcanic mountains and lava outcrops. Halfway along the coast between Morro beach and the city is the popular beach of Playa del Perchel.

WEST FROM PUERTO ROSARIO

If you take the coast road south from Puerto del Rosario you will pass the beach resort of **Castillo de Fustes** on the left, which was built around a 1740 watchtower. After this is the **Casa de las Salinas** (the old Salt House) which overlooks the early salt pans. After passing a number of ancient Guanche ruins on the left, follow the route to the old capital, Antigua. The old **Hermitage of San Francisco** is on the right. It roughly marks the centre of the island, which you will pass before reaching the 18th-century town of **Antigua**, situated on a parched plain and breaking the rugged skyline. This was once the island's capital and its charming whitewashed houses are a mixture of Moorish and Spanish architectural styles. The area around the town is famous for its many windmills. Stop for a meal at the 200-year-old **El Molino** round restaurant just outside the town and make a point of seeing the beautifully restored granary with its wooden ceiling.

> **MIGUEL DE UNAMUNO**
>
> Fuerteventura was used over the centuries as a place of exile for those who criticized the Spanish government. The writer and philosopher Miguel de Unamuno (1854–1936), however, seems to have rather enjoyed his brief exile here in 1924. Calling the island an 'oasis in the desert of civilization', 'a naked, arid, barren, bone-hard land which soothes the spirit', he obviously appreciated the solitude.

Betancuria **

In a magnificent mountain setting, Betancuria was named after the 15th-century Norman conqueror, Jean de Béthancourt, who built a fort as refuge from pirate

Above: *El Castillo (also known as Caleta de Fuste), a beach resort built around an 18th-century watch tower.*
Left: *Betancuria, a lovely old colonial town named after a 15th-century conquistador, Jean de Béthancourt, and once the island's capital.*

CINDER CULTIVATION

Fuerteventura is the driest of the Canary's seven islands. Less than 15cm (6in) of water falls here anually. The volcanic soil is rich. Apart from a few precious springs in the south, and some wells which produce brackish water, irrigation on the island has been the product of man's ingenuity. A certain type of volcanic cinder, mined in the north, was found to have properties which retain night mists and dews. By spreading this mineral on small stone-walled plots of land, terraced into the hillside, the islanders have been able to raise crops of cereals and vegetables. With the aqueous stratas increasingly eluding the reach of windmill bores, cistern ships supply the island with water from the mainland.

attacks. It is now a national monument and contains some interesting relics. Besides this monument there is also the **Museo Arqueológico,** housing artefacts dating back to Guanche times. Betancuria's church of **Santa María** is an architectural gem. The ceiling has wonderful decorated beams and the gilded high altar dates back to the 17th century.

Once the most important town in the Canary island group, Betancuria was incorporated into Spain's Crown of Castile in 1405, and its cathedral, **Iglesia Santa María de Betancuria**, formed the seat of the Lords of Fuerteventura. Béthancourt's standard can still be seen in the cathedral church, and the island's longest ruling families, the Saavedras, had their coat of arms engraved on the exterior of the church. This was once the island's cathedral until it was destroyed by pirates in 1539.

Valley of Palms **

The Valley of Palms, or the **Vega del Rio de Palmas**, lies in the shadow of the Hermitage and Sanctuary of the Virgen de Peña, Fuerteventura's patron saint. For absolute tranquillity and shade, this little oasis, which is dominated by the peak of **Gran Montana**, is unsurpassed on the island.

Iglesia de la Virgen de la Regla **

A short way south is the small, pretty village of **Pájara**, or 'Tiny Hen'. Dominating the square is a lovely church, the **Iglesia de la Virgen de la Regla**, which dates back to 1645. It has a charming interior with beautifully painted altar screens in a simple floral design. The church portal, which is believed to date from the 16th century, is executed in pink sandstone and carved with symbols of suns, snakes, lions and doves.

Below: *Animals are practical farming aids on Fuerteventura's terraced farms.*

Milling around Windmills

Heading east from Pájara, you'll find the village of **Tuineje**, with its many windmills which are well worth visiting. Windmills were used to grind the grain used for **gofio**, once the island's staple food. **Tiscamanita** has a well-preserved, three-storey windmill. A similar one with six sails can be viewed at **Llanos de la Concepción** and there are several at **Villaverde**.

There are interesting mills at **Lajares, El Cotillo** and **Carralejo**. A few have lost their outbuildings because the stone blocks have been used for houses or walls. Some are in working order but many need to be renovated. Lime kilns are often mistaken for windmill ruins, owing to the state of disrepair of many mills. You may find it difficult to distinguish which is which from a distance.

Above: *Windmills in the interior make practical use of the strong winds that blow across the island.*

SOUTH FROM PUERTO DEL ROSARIO

In order to reach the **Jandía Peninsula** which has more than half of the island's beaches, take the coastal road from Puerto del Rosario. This road passes the island's second port, **Gran Tarajal**. The peaks of the Jandía Peninsula here are just high enough to catch a little rain from the prevailing trade winds, sufficient to raise exportable quantities of tomatoes, shipped from this port. The road also passes the seaside resorts of **Tarajalejo** and **Playa Puerto Rico**. The longer, inland route is far more scenic. On your way back to Pájara, and then to **La Pared** village, you will notice that the scenery begins to change dramatically. Jagged gorges and volcanic cones become even more rugged as the road winds through one of the island's most isolated regions.

Passing through **Pájara**, historians will look in vain for traces of the mini-Hadrian's Wall which used to divide the twin kingdoms of the island in Guanche days. As you

Right: *Strong*
Atlantic breezes make
the Jandía Peninsula a
windsurfer's paradise.
Below: *Exotic fish swim*
in abundance in the azure
ocean waters.
Opposite: *Eye-catching*
replica of an old-fashioned
boat, half-buried in
the southern sands.

TOP TRIPS

Although Fuerteventura
appears barren and of little
interest on the face of it,
there are numerous trips
which reveal its hidden
secrets. From **Corralejo** you
could hop on a boat to **Wolf
Island** or do a day trip to
Lanzarote, or take a taxi
tour around Fuerteventura.
Big game fisherman can go
on a six-hour shark fishing
trip from the **Jandía Hotel**.

cross the ancient boundary between the kingdoms of Maxorata in the north, and that of Jandía in the south, the island's nickname of 'Solitude Isle' bites home. Entering the 'bottle neck' or isthmus of the Jandía Penininsula, the road after Pared turns east from the **Barlovento** (leeward) coast, and the Club Aldiana resort, towards the **Sotavento** (windward) beaches.

The desolate landscape on the way to Morro suddenly materializes into the spectacular vista of turquoise seas and the built-up resort area of **Matas Blancas** to the left. This is the well-known 25km (15 mile) beach lying to the north of the Sotavento coast. From here, picture-postcard beaches are fronted by tourist developments like the **Canada del Rio**, the **Costa Calma**, **Playa Esmeralda Jandía** and the vast sprawl of **Los Goriones**. The road takes you to the port town of **Morro del Jable** and steep cliffs start to line the beautiful coastline. This is an important commercial fishing port and its restaurants certainly confirm its commitment to maintaining the tradition of seafood menus. You will see crescents of sandy beaches on the left side of the road, while saw-toothed volcanic mountains provide a dramatic backdrop to the right. Smaller resorts include **Playa Juan Gomez** beaches and the villages of **Casa de Joros** and **Casa Cueva de la Negra**. The dominant shoreline feature is the **Playa de las Pillas**, a long stretch of beach running east to west along the southernmost point of the island.

Jandía Mountain **

As you head towards the tip of the island, the mountain, which rises like a pyramid inland is the 807m (2647ft) Jandía Mountain. This is Fuerteventura's highest point. The rocks here are some of the oldest in the entire Canarian archipelago.

Caserio Puerto de la Luz **

Near the southernmost tip of Fuerteventura is the lighthouse at Caserio Puerto de la Luz. This area, and the majority of the peninsula, was given to German engineer (and Nazi sympathizer) Gustave Winter by President Franco, for services rendered. Rumoured to have been in league with the Germans during World War II, Winter was later suspected of harbouring war criminals fleeing to South America. This region, and the Sotavento coastline, is a favourite holiday resort with German tourists. The coast is now a **national underwater park**.

The west coast, consisting of 20km (12½ miles) of white sandy beach and lying a couple of kilometres from the the giant resorts of the Sotavento coast, is virtually deserted, principally because it is difficult to get to. The Atlantic breezes have created some really magnificent beaches, such as the **Playa de Barlovento de Jandía** and the **Playa de Cofete**, which is quite near to an ancient abandoned hamlet. On this side of the peninsula the winds have carved weird and fantastic natural sculptures from the volcanic and sandstone cliffs which guard the shoreline.

Fuerteventura at a Glance

BEST TIMES TO VISIT

Fuerteventura has almost a North African climate: little variation in temperature year-round. Winter nights are cool, and a jacket is recommended.

GETTING THERE

Most visitors, except those from the Spanish mainland, arrive by air at **Los Estancas International Airport**, south of the capital. There are **ferry services** from Cádiz for passengers and cars to the island.

GETTING AROUND

The best way to get around is to hire a **car** and select where you want to go. You will need an international driving licence. Drive on the right. Seat belts are compulsory. Speed limits vary from 60kph (35mph) in built up areas, to 120kph (75mph) on motorways. Many petrol stations close on Sundays and few take credit cards. There is a **bus service**, but timetables are erratic. Travel agents can advise of bus times, and also organize a day's **taxi** tour of the island: a set package including lunch. Long-distance taxi rides have a set rate and short distances are metered.

WHERE TO STAY

Puerto del Rosario
LUXURY
Parador National de Fuerteventura, Playa Blanca; tel: (928) 85 11 50, fax: 85 11 58; near town, homely, in traditional Canarian setting.

BUDGET
Roquemar, Ruperto Gonzales Negrin 1; tel: (928) 85 03 59; basic facilities, central location.
Hotel Tamasite, Calle Léon y Castillo 9; tel: (928) 85 02 80; basic facilities, convenient.

Corralejo
LUXURY
Dunapark, General Franco, s/n; tel: (928) 53 52 51, fax: 53 54 91; central, excellent facilities, access for handicapped.

MID-RANGE
Apartamentos Corralejo Beach, Ave General Franco; tel: (928) 86 63 15, fax 86 63 17; excellent facilites.
Riu Palace Tres Islas, Playa de Corralejo; tel: (928) 53 57 00, fax (928) 53 58 58; on the beach, all rooms have terraces.

BUDGET
Corralejo Hotel, Calle Colon 12, Playa Corralejo; tel: (928) 53 52 46; basic, on the beach.
Riu Oliva Beach, Playa de Corralejo; tel: (928) 86 61 00; fax: (928) 86 61 54; Olympic-size pool, views of beach and sand dune park.

Jandía
LUXURY
Princesa Star, Avda. del Saladar, 28, Jandia-Pajara; tel: (928) 54 04 30, fax: 54 02 18; top hotel here, with all facilites.
Hotel Riu Calypso, Carr. General de Morro Jable; tel: (928) 54 00 26, fax: 54 07 30; excellent facilities, pool.

MID-RANGE
Apartamentos Atlantica, Avda. del Saladar 28, Jandia-Pajara; tel: (928) 87 60 17; good location with facilities.
Los Gorriones, Playa la Barca; tel: (928) 87 08 50; Jandia's first hotel with three pools.

BUDGET
Fiesta Casa Atlantica, Jandia Playa; tel: (928) 87 60 17; reasonable facilities, with all the basic requirements.

Canada del Rio (Pájara)
LUXURY
Riu Fuerteventura, Playa Urbanizacion Canada del Rio; tel: (928) 54 73 44; fax: 54 70 97; new four-star installation.
Sol Elite Gorriones, Playa Barca, s/n; tel: (928) 54 70 25, fax: 54 70 00; magnificent location with all facilities including pool and golf course.

MID-RANGE
Taro Beach, Urbanizacion Canada del Rio, Costa Calma-Pajara; tel: (928) 54 70 98, fax: 50 70 76; an excellent range of facilities but quite expensive.
Club Solyventura, tel: (928) 87 03 32, fax: 54 70 00; has a range of facilites, including a good swimming pool.

Antigua
MID-RANGE
Apartments El Castillo, Urbanizacion Castillo Caleta de Fustes; tel: (928) 87 81 00; beautifully located, chalet-type accommodation.

Fuerteventura at a Glance

La Oliva
MID-RANGE
Apartments Los Barqueros,
Avenida Grandes Playas, s/n;
tel: (928) 86 60 72; well-
serviced apartments.
Hotel Hopalco, Avenida
General Franco 45; tel: (928)
86 60 40; has very good
accommodation.

Corralejo
La Barca, Calle Generalisimo
Franco; tel: (928) 86 60 54;
tasty seafood dishes.
Casa de Candelaria, Calle
Almirante Carrero Blanco;
tel: (928) 86 60 97;
international cuisine.
Chato y Manuela, Calle Isaac
Peral; tel: (928) 86 62 86;
excellent local dishes.
La Taberna, Calle H. Cortez 3;
tel: (928) 53 50 27; typical
traditional fare.

Jandía
La Andaluza, Playa del
Matorral; tel: (928) 87 60 47;
great seafood selection.
Casa Juan, tel: (928) 87 63
60; local dishes, traditional.
El Meson, Playa Paradiso; tel:
(928) 54 02 03; range of dishes.
Taberna del Pescador, Playa
del Matorral; tel: (928) 87 64
11; Famous fish dishes.

Antigua
Casa Frasquita, Caleta de
Fustes; good local fare.
Molino Antigua, tel: (928) 87
82 20; interesting mill location,
good traditional fare.

La Oliva
Mariquito Hierro, Calle Maria
Hierro; tel: (928) 86 80 49
specializes in traditional food.

Although Fuerteventura
appears barren and of little
interest on the face of it, there
are numerous trips which
reveal its hidden secrets.
Northern Tour of the Island:
Ultramar Express, Hotel Rui
Oliva Beach, La Oliva, tel: (928)
86 62 51; or Viajes Canyrama,
Carretera Carrero Blanco,
tel: (928) 86 62 25.
**Western or Southern Round
Tour:** Viajes Insular, Avenida 1
de Mayo 52, Puerto del
Rosario, tel: (928) 85 05 94; or
Viajes Paukner, Avenida
Generalisimo, 34, La Oliva,
tel: (928) 86 60 10.
Lobos Island: visit from
Corralejo, taking one of the
day tours to Lanzarote, also
from Corralejo; Ultramar
Express, Hotel Rui Oliva Beach,
La Oliva, tel: (928) 86 62 51.
**Taxi tour of the island from
Corralejo:** Autos Estupinan,
Avenida Gernalisimo 18,
Corralijo, tel: (928) 86 60 48.
**Shark and deep-sea fishing
trips:** Escualo, Corralejo;

tel: (928) 85 13 29 or
Pez Verlero, Corralejo,
tel: (928) 86 61 73.
Round trip (windmills):
Viajes Elba, Carretera Princesa
Tamonante, Gran Tarajal,
Tuineji, tel: (928) 87 00 33.

**Corralejo: Barakuda Club,
Diving Centre**, tel: (928)
86 62 43.
Jandía: Aldiana Club,
tel: (928) 54 14 47.
**Antigua: El Castillo-
Caleta de Fustes**, tel: (928)
87 81 00/1.
Deep-sea Fishing: Escualo,
tel: (928) 85 13 29.
Pez Velero, tel: (928) 86 61 73.
Tourist Information Centre,
Avda 1 de Mayo 33, Puerto del
Rosario, tel/: (928) 85 10 24.
Cabildo Insular, Carretera
1 de Mayo 39, Puerto del
Rosario, tel: (928) 85 14 00.
Areopuerto Los Estancas
Puerto del Rosario, tel: (928)
85 12 50.
IBERIA Airways 23 de Mayo
11, Puerto del Rosario,
tel: (928) 85 08 02.
**Transmediterranea
Shipping**, Léon y Castillo
46, Puerto del Rosario,
tel: (928) 85 00 95.

FUERTEVENTURA	J	F	M	A	M	J	J	A	S	O	N	D
AVERAGE TEMP. °C	17	18	18	19	20	22	23	24	24	23	21	18
AVERAGE TEMP. °F	63	65	65	66	68	72	73	75	75	73	70	65
HOURS OF SUN DAILY	6	8	7	7	8	10	10	8	6	6	5	5
RAINFALL mm	36	8	2	11	2	0	0	0	6	3	58	9
RAINFALL in	1.5	0	0	0	0	0	0	0	0	0	2	0
DAYS OF RAINFALL	7	6	5	4	2	1	1	1	2	6	10	9

5
Lanzarote

Battered and scarred by the ravages of nature, Lanzarote is the Canaries' fourth largest island. There are over 300 volcanoes sprinkled throughout the island and in 1730 a six-year period of eruptions began, transforming the face of Lanzarote. A quarter of the island was blanketed with ash and the surface sculpted into the desolate, pock-marked landscape that exists today.

Lanzarote is a hauntingly beautiful island, unspoilt by rampant commercialism or insensitive development. The island is dotted with installations by artist César Manrique such as the **Mirador del Rio** and **Jameos del Agua** that imaginatively, yet sensitively, exploit the landscape without spoiling its charm. Islanders themselves are very environmentally aware and there are no high-rise concrete jungles to mar Lanzarote's natural beauty.

Surprisingly enough the land is fertile and prosperous, due to the *eneranado* water conservation method and cultivation of lava soil. Intricate arcs of rock and cinder terraces provide perfect conditions for growing vegetables, fruit and vines. **Malmsey wine** is an island speciality, a sweet yet sublime treat.

Today's tourists converge on **Timanfaya National Park** to explore the lava flows and experience the sheer force of nature. Fabulous beaches, picturesque villages and historic monuments all add to Lanzarote's charm. Off the island's northern tip is La Graciosa, a tranquil, rocky outcrop popular with fishermen and sun-worshippers.

DON'T MISS

*** **Timanfaya National Park:** eerie lunar landscape.
*** **Jameos del Agua** and **Cueva Los Verdes:** fascinating volcanic caverns.
*** **Mirador del Rio:** glorious views over La Graciosa.
*** **El Golfo:** luminous green lagoon inside a broken volcano cone.
** **Santa Barbara Fort:** near Teguise, dating from the 14th century.

Opposite: *Sunset lights up the Mountains of Fire in the Timanfaya National Park, a volcanic wilderness.*

EARLY HISTORY

King Juba II of Mauretania, West Africa, visited the island in the 1st century AD and reports about the islands were circulated by **Pliny the Elder**, who called Lanzarote and Fuerteventura *purpurariae*, after the purple dye produced from the local *orchilla* lichen. The first attempt at settlement was made by Arab explorers who, after subduing the local inhabitants, built a fort in the centre of the island in the 10th century. Around 300 years later in 1312, the Genoese **Lanzarotto Malocello** led an expedition here, calling the island after himself, and claiming it for Portugal. Spain arrived in the form of

Fernando Peraza's troops, who sacked the island in 1385, only to be followed by the Norman invasion of **Gadafir de la Salle** and **Jean de Béthancourt** in 1402. The family of **Diego de Herrera** ruled Lanzarote for most of the 15th century and it was incorporated into the Spanish crown in 1479. The 16th and 17th centuries saw a succession of pirate attacks, and the population waxed and waned throughout the 19th century. Tourism proper on Lanzarote began in the 1970s and has since become the island's main foreign currency earner.

ARRECIFE

Lanzarote's capital, Arrecife, is located about halfway along the east coast, facing south. Its name comes from the reefs and islets which are dotted throughout the wide bay. This is the closest port of the Canary Islands to the Saharan coast of Africa, and its fishing fleet benefits from the mainland's prolific fishing grounds. Until about 200 years ago, Teguise was the capital of Lanzarote. Consequently, Arrecife, in those days little more than a quiet coastal fishing port, has few of the historic attractions of the original capital.

Fort of San Gabriel **

The two prominent sites of this rather bland capital are the forts of **San Gabriel** and **San José**, standing at either side of the arm of the bustling harbour. Designed by

Above: *Umbrellas and sunloungers line the beach at Puerto del Carmen, Lanzarote's most popular resort.*
Below: *Ancient cannon guard the fortress walls of San Gabriel in Arrecife.*

Right: *César Manrique's 1968 museum and rural restaurant is located in the geographical centre of Lanzarote.*

the island's first prison governor, Don Gaspar de Salcedo, in 1573, the Fortress of San Gabriel was burnt down in an attack on the natural harbour in 1586. The Italian engineer and architect to Felipe II, Leonardo Torriani, rebuilt the fort and reclad its four diamond-shaped corners in 1590. Today, the castle houses a small **Archaeological Museum**. A drawbridge, the **Puente de las Bolas**, links the El Quemado promontory on which the fort stands with the centre of the town. Open 9:00–13:00 and 15:00–18:00 daily.

MOST FAMOUS SON

Lanzarote's most famous citizen was the architect, painter and sculptor **César Manrique** (1920–1992). He wanted to protect his island from over-development and thought that architecture made from natural materials should exist in harmony with the environment. It's largely thanks to him that Lanzarote has been spared the horrors of high-rises and garish advertising.

Fort of San José ★★★
Standing between the Los Marmoles breakwater and El Puerto del Naos, to the north of the town, the 1799 Castillo de San José, built during Carlos III's reign, contains the **Museum of Contemporary Art**, with works by modern masters Picasso, Miró and the celebrated local artist, César Manrique. Above the dungeon art galley there is a good restaurant and bar.

Manrique's gallery is on Calle José Béthencourt and is one of the artist's famous murals. It is made from local lava and decorates the foyer of the old Gran Hotel, which still dominates Arrecife's harbourside skyline.

The town's pretty Municipal Park is also the work of César Manrique, and well worth a visit. The main church in the town is **San Gines** and the patron saint's day is on 25 August, an exuberant fiesta with fireworks, music and a camel parade.

Arrecife has three beaches: **Playa Blanca**, **El Reducto** and **Guacineta**. The only commercial airport on the island is about 6km (4 miles) south of Arrecife town, past the resort of **Playa Honda**. Playa El Reducto, situated just south of Arrecife, is the town's best beach.

TIMANFAYA NATIONAL PARK

It takes about three hours to do a complete tour of Timanfaya Park, an atmospheric volcanic wilderness created during the 18th-century eruptions. A visit to the park must be done through the organized tourist routes as it is forbidden to enter the area unaccompanied. Approach the **Montañas del Fuego** (Mountains of Fire) of the volcanic area of Timanfaya by way of the picturesque village of **Yaiza**. The entrance to the park is signposted with the National Park emblem of a devil waving a pitchfork. One of the best ways of exploring the park is on a camel and there are regular excursions which leave from Uga village. It pays to bear in mind that camels are rather uncomfortable, noisy, smelly beasts with unbelievably bad breath!

PLAYING WITH FIRE

Lanzarote is famed for its novel, natural ovens. The area is known as the Timanfaya, and the cooking site is in the **Montañas del Fuego**, or Mountains of Fire. A few centimetres below ground, the volcanic activity can range from 100° to over 400°C (752°F) on the hillock of **Tinecheide**. Potatoes can be baked in the soil here, and local guides demonstrate the various wonders of the fearful land which bubbles in molten frenzy just a short distance under the visitor's feet. The mountain of Timanfaya, which gave its name to the area, is an extinct volcanic cone which rises to 510m (1673ft) and can be reached by camels which are provided locally.

Below: *Camel treks are a novel way of exploring Timanfaya's lava flows.*

SALT OF THE SEA

Salt, an important commodity, especially in the early days when meat had to be preserved, became a major industry in Lanzarote when the economy dwindled during the mid-19th century. Today, three major salt pan areas still produce salt at **Janubio**, the **Salinas del Rio**, and north of Arrecife. The large works at **El Charco** has now been developed for tourism. More than 10,000 tonnes are extracted from sea water each year and are used to salt down fish. The salt pans of the Salinas del Rio are pink, attributed to the minute salt water shrimps which attract flocks of flamingo. Lanzarote is the only Canary island to produce salt, although the salt houses at the **Salinas del Carmen**, on Fuerteventura, stand testament to its past industry.

Near the Islote de Hilario parking lot, named after a hermit who lived alone on this spot for 50 years with just a donkey as company, is the **El Diablo** (Devil) Restaurant. This interesting building was designed in glass and lava by César Manrique. Meals in the restaurant are cooked over the natural volcanic heat. The temperature, just below the surface, is demonstrated outside the restaurant by guides who conduct various experiments showing how brushwood fed into a hole instantly bursts into flame, and water is turned into an explosion of steam.

Take the opportunity to go on the spectacular hourly **Lunar Ride** by coach up into the multi-coloured volcanic *malpaís* (badlands) to look into smoking craters and for views across the desert-like moonscape to the distant farms and the sea. Unfortunately, it is forbidden to take samples of volcanic rock from the park.

THE SOUTHERN ROUTE

Some visitors prefer to see the volcanic region at sunset, because of the fantastic colours produced by the rays of the sinking sun. Whether taking the morning or evening tour it's well worthwhile combining your visit to the Timanfaya Park with a trip around the south of the island. Out of **Puerto del Carmen**, the road runs through the **La Geria** wine-producing region. It then passes

Below: *Malpaís, or badlands territory in Timanfaya.*

through **Uga** village, reconstructed 10m (33ft) above the original village, which was buried in the volcanic eruptions of 1730. The flat roofs of the whitewashed houses here are designed to catch precious rainwater. See the sloping-sided little church of **San Isidro Labrador** and the exhibitions of Canarian wrestling at the Timanfaya Restaurant. The next town on the route to the west coast is **Yaiza**, said to be the most typical of all settlements on Lanzarote. The village square and 18th-century church of **Los Remedios** are extremely photogenic, as are the **Jardínes de la Era**.

Take the road south, towards the salt pans. A side road branches off to the beautiful bay of **El Golfo**, nestling in the half-moon remnants of a volcanic crater. The Salinas de Janubio, the desalination plant, is one of Lanzarote's trademarks and produces around 10,000 tonnes of salt a year which is used for preserving fish. The process of evaporation takes about four weeks. Vast checkerboard patterns of the flat salt pans are dotted with little pyramids of sea salt.

An irridescent turquoise lagoon beyond the salt pans is a haven for a variety of birds. The main road now runs south, to the beach resort of **Playa Blanca**. This was once a small fishing village but is now a thriving resort giving access to more beaches at **Papagayo**. The ferry to and from Puerto del Rosario and Fuerteventura runs from Playa Blanca.

A CENTRAL ROUTE

For six years after a tremendous volcanic eruption and earthquake ripped the heart out of Lanzarote in 1730, lava flows and ash and cinder fallout blanketed the land. A four-hour central island walk of around 13km (8 miles) will give you an insight into the extent of the holocaust. Starting off from **Uga**, at the heart of the **La Geria** wine region, after taking the Playa Blanca bus from Puerto del

Above: *The ferry to Fuerteventura leaves from the fast-growing resort of Playa Blanca.*

A LIMPID, LANGUID LAGOON

On the southwest coast of Lanzarote the visitor follows contorted lava which flows down to a spectacular, crescent-shaped lagoon. **El Golfo** lies in the remains of a half-eroded volcanic cone, forming a semi-circular amphitheatre around a vast pool. The inside of the crater has been terraced by wind and sea, and the noise of the nearby surf echoes around the natural auditorium. A unique mollusc, the clico, lives in the salt water of El Golfo. Salt is an important part of the economy here, as the huge salt pans of nearby **Janubio** show.

CULTIVATING CLOUDS

Few clouds break over this desert land but the ingenious islanders have developed a method of harvesting the moisture-laden trade winds. After the devastation of the 1730–36 volcanic eruptions, it looked as though Lanzarote would remain barren. Farmers, however, invented a unique system of man-made craters, surrounded by lava rock walls which, at night, trap the moisture in the air to feed the plants, vegetables, figs and vines which are planted in the 2.5m (8ft) diameter hollows. The low stone walls also protect the plants, creating a unique landscape. It looks as though the vines that produce the island's excellent Malmsey wine grow straight out of the black sand soil.

Carmen, walk through the village past the Timanfaya Restaurant and turn left at the sign 'Teguise por la Geria'. Uga is also the base for the Timanfaya camel tours. Pass two houses before turning right up the next track and look for a yellow-topped marker post. Continue right with **Mount Guardilama** in front, through vineyards enclosed by numerous hand-built stone walls. Take a left turn at the summit of the pass, where the vineyards come to an end. Take a short hike to the top of the slippery cindered Mount Guardilama for panoramic views over a blackened landscape. The land is pock-marked with crescent-shaped sheltering walls with a background of hazy volcanic cones, as well as the far arc of a white-fringed coastline. Head down along the main track keeping **La Asomada** village to the left, turning a short distance after the white building to the right.

Take a left turn at **Caminos los Olivos** and right at **Camino la Calderina** to the GC720 main road. Pass **Macher** village windmill, turning to the right and take a dirt track towards the sea. This passes Casa Romerito and if you turn left at Camino del Puerto it'll take you to the road leading back to **Puerto del Carmen**.

Left: *Musicians performing at Teguise play the timple, a small instrument similar to a ukelele.*

Opposite: *The crescent-shaped terraces of La Geria, Lanzarote's wine-growing region, are known as 'zocos'.*

TEGUISE

Often known as 'La Villa', this was the original capital of the island, a title transferred in 1852 to the port of Arrecife. Teguise is the first European town in the Canaries, and was founded by Maciot de Béthancourt, the nephew of the conquistador Jean de Béthancourt. Maciot married the daughter of Guadarfia, the last native king of the island. Teguise is named after the Guanche princess and dates back to the 10th century. The town was set back from the coast in order to avoid attacks by marauding pirates.

Santa Barbara Fort *

Although it used to be called Guanapay, the castle is currently referred to as the Santa Barbara Fort, and was originally constructed in the 14th century by Lanzarotto Malocello. Sites in the town which evoke its erratic history include the **Callejon de la Sandre** (Blood Alley), named after the incessant attacks by Moors and Berbers.

Palace of Queen Ico **

In the old part of the town is the Palace of Queen Ico, the most beautiful historic house in the town. It used to be the residence of the **Marquis de Herrera**, a wealthy Genoese merchant who lived here with his family during the 18th century. It is now a museum. Other places to see include the lovely old churches and convents of **San Francisco**, **Vera Cruz** and **Santo Domingo**.

MOUNTAIN RIDES

Many beach resorts on the islands are geared up for excursions into the interior. These can take the form of overland four-wheel-drive safaris, often organized in convoys of trucks or jeeps, making a full or half-day trek over rugged terrain. Several islands have camel, donkey and horse centres where rides are organized into the hinterland.

UNDERGROUND WONDERLAND

In the **Malpaís de La Corona**, to the north of Lanzarote, is a remarkable rock formation created by explosive volcanic gases and molten lava. This is the longest known volcanic cave in the world and was once used as a refuge from Barbary pirates. The shorter **Jameos de Agua** cave formation contains an underground salt-water lagoon and gases have penetrated the cave roof, providing natural lighting. In 1976 **César Manrique** built an 800-seat underground auditorium inside the cavern, making use of the excellent subterranean acoustics.

Opposite: *Village and palm grove of La Haria, surrounded by volcanic cones.*
Below: *Striking cacti are the star attractions of the Jardín de Cactus, created by César Manrique.*

Nuestra Señora de Gualdeloupe ★★

The church of Nuestra Señora de Gualdeloupe, in the centre of Teguise, is one of the oldest in the Canaries. Typically Moorish-style grand houses and mansions with ornate balconies and shady courtyards dot the town's cobbled lanes.

El Meson de Paco ★★

The early 18th-century El Meson de Paco is just one of these grandiose houses, and it has been converted into a restaurant and art gallery. Teguise is an extensive municipality of Lazarote and includes 20 villages.

AROUND THE NORTH

Take the route out of the capital to **Tahiche**, a town with several imposing villas. One of these was the home of the artist César Manrique and is now a museum. Turning right, the road heads north to **Guatiza**, the cochineal centre of the island. Note the huge fields of optunia cactus, grown for the raising of the insect from which the red cochineal dye is extracted. Look for the windmill which has been converted into a restaurant as there is a fascinating **Cactus Garden** there.

Further north, the village of **Mala** is also a cochineal centre, but continue north, detouring to the right to visit the charming fishing port of **Arrieta**, with its black clinker beach.

Jameos del Agua ***

From here, a route heads out along the coast towards the Jameos del Agua cavern and the **Cueva de los Verdes**. The caves were created about 5000 years ago by exploding volcanic gases and lava which formed tunnels from Monte Corona to the sea. These caves were used as places of refuge by pirates. Returning to the main road, continue to the village of **Ye**, a word which means 'the end of the earth'. Once the centre for the production of purple dye, extracted from the orchilla lichen, it is now famed for the fabulous viewpoints located nearby.

Mirador del Rio ***

The road terminates on a flat plateau in the extreme north of the island, dominated by another of César Manrique's lava creations, the Mirador del Rio. Inland, there are marvellous views of the **Monte Corona** volcanic crater, and to the north there is a panoramic view over the El Rio stretch of sea between Lanzarote and the isle of Graciosa.

Haria *

Returning to Ye, take the route south, to pass through the **Valley of a Thousand Palms**, and Haria village. The capital of the northern province, Haria is a picturesque Moorish-style oasis, set in countryside which boasts the most palms in the entire Canary archipelago.

Above: *A typically white-washed villa, La Haria, covered with dazzling exotic blooms.*

Riscos de Famara ★★

Heading south again, the road passes the Riscos de Famara cliffs which rise at the island's highest point, the **Penas del Chache**, 670m (2198ft) above sea level. The land around the village of **Los Valles de Santa Catalina** is a highly fertile agricultural region. The road now runs through Teguise back to Arrecife.

LA GRACIOSA

This small, oblong-shaped islet is in the Minor Archipelago, a group which includes Alegranza, Montaña Clara, and the outcrop of Infierno (Hell's Rock or the Roque del Oeste) is just 27km² (10½ sq miles). La Graciosa lies to the north of Lanzarote and is separated from the larger island by a narrow stretch of water known as **El Rio** (The River). Inland, the terrain is bleak and barren. Among the four mountain peaks, the highest point, the **Montaña de las Aguilas** (The Needles) rises to 266m (873ft) above sea level in the centre of Graciosa. North of this is the 157m (515ft) **Montaña Bermeja**, and in the far south is the **Montaña Amarilla** (Yellow Mountain), just 172m (564ft) high.

On the east side of the island is the harbour of **Caleta del Sebo**, facing the **Salinas del Rio** on Lanzarote. Graciosa's only other settlement, a small fishing village called **Pedro Barba**, is located in the northeast of the island. Caleta del Sebo is over-shadowed by the **Montaña de Mojón**. The few volcanic cones on La Graciosa are surrounded by a flat, sandy plain. Around 500 people live on the island permanently. For many years the islanders depended entirely on fishing for their living. When a Canarian Governor named Garcia arrived in the 1850s. He divided the land between the inhabitants and gave them a dozen camels to boot! Since then, the Graciosans began farming what fertile land they could salvage.

Jean de Béthancourt claimed the island for the Spanish crown in 1402, when he landed there. He used this island as a military base from which he could attack the other islands. On hearing that Béthancourt's nephew, a few years later, was planning to sell La Graciosa to the Portugese, Juan II of Spain sent Pedro Barba to the island where he audaciously declared himself King of the Canaries. Cervantes refers to the incident in his novel, *Don Quixote*.

Below: *View of Isla Graciosa from Mirador del Rio.*

This little desert island was later to become the haunt of many pirates, with stories of buried buccaneers' treasure. The island now attracts fishermen and beach-lovers who flock to **Las Conchas** on the northwest coast, sheltered by the Montaña Bermeja, **Playa Lambra** in the north, **Playa Francesa** in the extreme south and the beach near the island's harbour.

AFRICA'S SHORES

From La Graciosa and Lanzarote, the shores of Morocco are just 100km (60 miles) to the east. You can make a flying visit from either Las Palmas's Gando Airport on Gran Canaria, or Reina Sofía Airport on Tenerife, to several destinations in West Africa. Morocco, Marrakesh, Casablanca, Agadir and El Aiun are the most popular destinations while excursions further abroad can be made to Nouadihbou and Nouakchott in Mauritania; to Dakar in Senegal, Libreville in Gabon and to Abijan on the Ivory Coast. There is a shipping line which takes passengers on the 18-hour sailing trip from Las Palmas to Agadir.

Lanzarote at a Glance

BEST TIMES TO VISIT

The climate varies little throughout the year, but at night, during the winter, the temperatures can drop and it may feel rather cool.

GETTING THERE

To Lanzarote: most visitors from abroad arrive by **air** at the **Arrecife Airport**. There are **ferry services** from Cádiz. **To La Graciosa:** a 40-minute **ferry** which leaves at 10:00 and returns around 16:00, runs between Orzola, at the northernmost tip of Lanzarote, and Caleta del Sebo.

GETTING AROUND

The best way to get around Lanzarote is by **car**. Petrol stations rarely accept credit cards and may be closed on Sundays. If you have brought you own car on the ferry, make sure you have the right documents. There are numerous **bus** excursions on the island with full or half day tours on offer.

WHERE TO STAY

There are only a few hotels on Lanzarote because most tourists prefer **apartment** blocks, or the cheaper **pensions**. On La Graciosa there is no official accommodation.

Arrecife
MID-RANGE
Miramar, Coll 2; tel: (928) 81 04 38, fax: 81 33 66; the facilities are basic but accommodation is near the town.

BUDGET
Cardona, Calle 18 de Julio 11; tel: (928) 81 10 08, fax: 81 70 08; comfortable pension-style accommodation offering adequate facilities.

Puerto del Carmen
LUXURY
Los Fariones, Roque del Este, 1; tel: (928) 51 01 75, fax: 51 02 02; great position, fine pool.

MID-RANGE
San Antonio, Avenida de las Playas 84; tel: (928) 51 42 00, fax: 51 30 80; quiet, 15 minutes from the airport.

Teguise
LUXURY
Gran Melia Salinas, Costa Teguise; tel: (928) 59 00 10, fax: 59 03 90; tropical-style hotel, sea views.

MID-RANGE
Occidental Teguise Playa, Avda. Jablillo, s/n; tel: (928) 59 06 54, fax: 59 09 79; private beach.

Yaiza
LUXURY
Hotel Lanzarote, Princess, Playa Blanca, Yaiza; tel: (928) 51 71 08, fax: 51 70 11; swimming pool.

MID-RANGE
Hotel Playa Flamingo, Urbanizacion Montana Roja; tel: (928) 51 73 00, fax: 51 76 42; bungalows in lovely garden location, pool, artificial beach.

Tias
LUXURY
Riu Palace Lanzarote, Playa de los Pocillos, tel: (928) 51 24 04, fax: 51 35 98; good amenities, pool.

BUDGET
Magec, Calle Hierro 8; tel: (928) 51 38 74; basic pension-style accommodation.

Apartments
Arrecife
MID-RANGE
Arrecife Playa, Avenida Mancomunidad 4; tel: (928) 81 03 00, fax: 81 39 37; quite convenient location.

BUDGET
Apartamentos Islamar, Avda. Rafael Gonzalez Negrin 15; tel: (928) 81 15 04, fax: 81 15 00; centrally located in the city on the edge of the main park.

Puerto del Carmen
LUXURY
Apartementos Flamingo Club, Avenida Las Playas; tel: (928) 51 27 53, fax: 51 43 70; great for families.

MID-RANGE
Apartamentos Morana, Guanapay 2; tel: (928) 51 01 93, fax: 51 27 24; economical, mid-1980s style.
Apartamentos Kontiki, Guanapay 5; tel: (928) 51 39 50, fax: 51 39 77; popular, central.
Apartamentos Las Panitas y Las Calas, Cla Chalana 2; tel:

Lanzarote at a Glance

(928) 51 42 62, fax: 51 42 63; central in resort.
Apartamentos Playa Club, Pedro Barba 2; tel: (928) 51 37 19, fax: 51 09 06; economical.

WHERE TO EAT

Arrecife
Juan Carlos, Calle José Antonio 100; traditional fare.

Tias
Castillo San José, modern furnishing inside a fascinating old castle.Well worth a visit.

Puerto del Carmen
Casa Colón, Centro Comercial Matagorda; tel: (928) 51 25 54; fresh fish and traditional dishes.

Yaiza
Chu-Lin 1V, Playa Blanca; tel: (928) 51 75 67; roast pork dishes are a speciality here.

Timanfaya National Park
El Diablo; tel: (928) 84 00 56; watch dishes being cooked in the hot lava ovens.
Castillo de San José; tel: (928) 81 23 21; castle and museum with restaurant and exhibition centre. Open 11:00–21:00, daily. Restaurant opens 13:00–16:00 and 20:00–01:00.

TOURS AND EXCURSIONS

Jeep Excursions: most major hotels can organize jeep safaris on the island. Pick-up points are generally in the Teguise resort area, at points in the Puerto del Carmen resort and in Arrecife. Tours start between

08:30 and 09:30 depending on the pick-up point. Often the tours are in convoy. Contact Explora (tel: (928) 81 36 42), the major excursion company.
Timanfaya National Park: conducted bus tours leave from the entrance hourly, and independent visits can be made only with an authorized guide, tel: (928) 84 00 57 for the Park's organizers. Open 09:00-17:45.
Jameos del Agua: the lava grotto in the northeast of the island offers a guided tour and has a restaurant, tel: (928) 84 80 04 for details. Open 11:00–18:45 daily. For events held in the caves, it opens again 19:00–03:00 on Tues, Fri and Sat.
Cueva de los Verdes: conducted tours take visitors through this cave system in the northeast of Lanzarote every hour from 10:20 until 18:00. So popular is this attraction that it is advisable to go early as the caves quickly become far too busy; tel: (928) 17 32 20 for details.
Mirador del Rio: the observation gallery with its bar and café on the extreme northernmost point of the island overlooks La Graciosa Island. Open to visitors from 10:30 until 18:45 daily, tel: (928) 61 43 18 for further information.
Boat Trips: various excursions leave regularly from Arrecife, Puerto del Carmen and Playa Blanca. Trips can be made to the Islands of Lobos and Fuerteventura. A sailing trip offers excursions from Arrecife,

down Lanzarote's east coast as far as Papagayo, in the far south and back to the port.
Coach Excursions: there are numerous coach trips which can be joined at many of the larger hotels and apartment complexes. The full day trip to Timanfaya Park is popular. This excursion also takes in the sites of El Golfo, La Geria and Yaiza. Alternatively, there is a half-day tour to the north of the island which includes Teguise, Haria, the Mirador del Rio, the Cueva de los Verdes and the Jameos del Agua. More specialist trips take visitors to see Canarian wrestling and traditional folk dancing displays at Uga or to the Teguise market on Sundays.
Sport: Tennis and watersport facilities are available at most apartment complexes and hotels. There are special centres for sports such as squash, basketball, volleyball, windsurfing and scuba diving.

USEFUL CONTACTS

Tourist Information Office, Parque José Ramírez Cerda, tel/fax: 81 18 60; Internet: www.cabildo.com
Patronato de Turismo, Antiguo Parador de Turismo, Arrecife, tel: (928) 81 17 62.
Aeropuerto de Lanzarote, Arrecife, tel: (928) 81 03 50.
IBERIA Airlines, Avenida Rafael Gonzalez 2, Arrecife, tel: (928) 81 61 08.
Betancuria Ferry, tel: (928) 51 72 66.

6
Tenerife

This is probably the best known of all the Canary Islands. Tenerife is the largest island in the archipelago and boasts the highest point in Spain, **Mount Teide**, which is 3718m (12,198ft) high. Locals call Tenerife the '**Island of Eternal Spring**'. Green acres of banana plantations, oranges, fields of tomatoes and, lately, other tropical fruits endorse this title, as do the green northern regions and the island's perfect climate.

A rocky spine runs down the isle to Mount Teide, which is surrounded by an enormous crater known as **Las Cañadas**; together they form Teide National Park. The volcano has been dormant as far back as 1798 and the mountain is still easily reached by road or by cable car.

The **Anaga Mountains** shelter the capital, **Santa Cruz**, on the rugged northern tip of the island. In the west are the remote **Teno Hills**. Both north and west are the most fertile and green regions, compared with the rather dull and dry southern part of Tenerife, where holidaymakers crowd onto beaches such as **Playa de las Américas** and **Los Cristianos**. Near these popular resorts is the **Costa del Silencio**, with breathtaking views of **Punta de la Rasca**, the island's southernmost point. **Las Teresitas**, north of the capital, is famous for its large artificial beach of Saharan sands.

Away from the resorts are numerous lovely old towns full of historic buildings and tranquil, leafy squares. **La Laguna**, **Orotava** and **Puerto de la Cruz** in particular are charming colonial towns.

Don't Miss

*** La Laguna: original settlement with many fine religious monuments and historic sites.
*** La Orotava: grand old town houses and a 16th-century church.
*** Mount Teide: highest peak in Spain and massive crater 80km (50 miles) across.
*** Icod: see the ancient dragon tree and views of Mount Teide.

Opposite: *Viewed across the lava-based town of Garachico is the pinnacle of the Roque de Garachico.*

Tenerife

CRIME

Theft from cars is by far the
most common crime:you can
virtually guarantee having
your car broken into if you
park overnight in the streets
of one of the big towns or
resorts. Don't leave anything
of value in your car, even if
it is locked in the boot. If
you are burgled, you'll need
a report from the local police
station for insurance purposes. In cities and resorts
there are the usual problems
of bag-snatching and occasional muggings in the seedier
areas. Be as street-wise as
you'd be in your own country.

SANTA CRUZ DE TENERIFE

Located on the northeast coast of Tenerife, the capital is a
bustling city and major commercial and cruise ship port,
quite different from anywhere else on the island. Santa
Cruz is also the administrative capital of the four
Western Islands of the Canaries. It is situated on a large
natural bay, with a backdrop of the 1000m (3281ft) high
Anaga mountains. A small gorge, the **Barranco de
Santos,** runs through part of the city. Santa Cruz rarely
holds visitors' attention for long, as most tourists head
for the beach resorts or natural attractions of the countryside. The city is famous for its extravagant carnival
usually held in February, depending on the dates of Lent.

The capital has over 203,000 inhabitants, roughly a
third of the island's population, and it is one of Spain's
busiest harbours, having attained freeport status in 1852.

It is also one of the deepest ports in the world. Today, few traces remain of the city's early history.

Tourism first started in Tenerife in 1886 when Bernard Walsh opened the **Grand Hotel** in **Puerto de la Cruz**, which is situated on the other side of the island. It was usual for tourism to start in the capital, but this was not the case for Tenerife. From the mid-19th century, the island's capital, however, became an important commercial centre. Today, most travellers to Tenerife arrive at the **Reina Sofía International Airport** in the south of the island. The city itself has many attractions, and most visitors start their tour of the city's main sights from the portside corniche.

City Sightseeing

There are several points of interest in this largely modern city. The **Plaza de España** is the main feature of the seafront and a good place to start a tour of the city; there's also a car park nearby. Towering over the circular Plaza is the **Monumento de los Caidos**, commemorating those who died in the Spanish Civil War (1936–39). The large building facing the monument is the **Palacio Insular**, the house of the government of Tenerife. The foyer has a fine relief model of the entire island, which is useful for visitors who wish to see the island in perspective and plan excursions. The **Island Tourist Board** is also located here, where you can pick up maps, street plans, information on accommodation and transport timetables.

Around the corner from the Tourist Office, the nearest museum to the Plaza de España is the **Archaeological and Anthropological Museum** situated on Avenida Bravo Murillo, on the second floor of the

Below: *The Canary Islands are well known for the excellence of their pot-tery and tile craftsmanship both for decorative and practical use. These bench-brick advertising plaques, in Plaza 25 Julio in Santa Cruz de Tenerife, serve both purposes.*

CHILDREN

Tenerife, Gran Canaria and Lanzarote are ideal for family holidays. Canarians love children and you'll have no problems taking them into restaurants or bars. There are plenty of watersports, water-parks, go-karts, several wildlife parks and camel or donkey rides for children to enjoy.

Palacio Insular. This museum has an excellent collection of artifacts from Guanche times. Exhibits include mummified Guanches (once stored in caves), weapons, tools, cooking utensils and early jewellery. Open 09:00–13:00 and 16:00–18:00, Monday–Friday, 09:00–13:00 Saturday, tel: (928) 60 55 74.

Just inland from the Plaza de España is the Plaza de Candelaria. Here the 1742 **Palacio de Carta** bank, a National Monument, is a fine example of colonial architecture. The nearby **Fine Arts Museum** is the city's main art gallery. Apart from the fabulous paintings there are also other fascinating things to see such as armour and

Santa Cruz de Tenerife

weaponry, ship models and coins. The museum is in the Plaza del Principe, a lovely leafy square. Open 10:00–20:00 (summer) 10:00–19:00 (winter), closed Friday and Sunday, tel: (928) 24 43 58. Behind this museum, facing on to the street below, is the beautiful Baroque 17th-century **Church of San Francisco**, which was founded by exiled Irish Catholics and which contains some fine sculptures.

Crossing into Plaza del Principe, the road running north is Calle del Pilar, named after the 18th-century **Church of Pilar**, worth seeing for its beautifully painted ceiling. At the top of Calle del Pilar are the charming landscaped gardens of **Jardín Garcia Sanabria**. Sculptures line the walks, together with finely tiled benches dating back to the park's foundation in the 1920s.

Above: *The Plaza de General Weyler, decked with colourful flowerbeds.*

To the west of the Plaza de España is the Church of **Nuestra Señora de la Concepción** on Plaza de la Iglesia. Built originally in 1502, the church was reconstructed after a fire in 1652. Its black and white tower is Moorish in influence. Inside the high Baroque interior, with its five naves, is a magnificent altarpiece, the Cross of Conquest, carried by Alonso de Lugo's men in 1494 , and the flags captured from Nelson's troops in 1797. Open 11:00–13:00, Monday–Friday. The nearby **Museum of Natural Science** is open 10:00–17:00 Tuesday–Saturday, tel: (928) 21 30 00.

Military Museum *

East of the city is the **Aimeyda Barracks**. Inside this is the Military Museum. Armour and weapons are exhibited here, some dating back to the conquistadores who defeated the Guanches in 1494. The prime exhibit is *El Tigre*, the cannon which was said to have torn Nelson's arm off in his failed attack on the city in 1797. The flags from HMS *Emerald*, the Admiral's flagship, are also on display here.

GETTING THE SACK

Shakespeare's Falstaff was probably the best-known imbiber of Canarian Sack or Malvasia (Malmsey) wine. This was one of the island's main exports to Europe from the 16th to the 18th centuries. Today this wine is still served. Other wines made on Tenerife include the celebrated Vino Norte, made in El Suazal. In most shops wines from other islands, like the Vino del Monte from Gran Canaria, or Vino Herreño from El Hierro, as well as Rioja imported from Spain, are becoming much more popular than the local Sack.

Shopping

Santa Cruz is a duty-free paradise for shopaholics. Just start at the **Plaza de España** and walk through to the **Plaza de la Candeleria**. The marble statue, carved by Canova in 1778, commemorates the Virgin of Candelaria. Change your money in the beautiful **Palacio de Carta** bank. Around the square is a jumble of shops, competing in price with each other, and selling a variety of similar goods. Arts and craftwork, ceramics and souvenirs, can be bought in the shops nearby, and leather boutiques and electrical shops line both sides of the street. Off the plaza, **Calle del Castillo** is Santa Cruz's main shopping thoroughfare.

DUTY-FREE SOUVENIRS

The best bargains in Tenerife are not the electrical goods or cameras, but alcohol, tobacco and craftwork. Buy these before leaving for the airport. In the island's main markets, like the Nuestra Señora de Africa in Santa Cruz, bargaining is recommended. Food produce, like local cheeses, honey, wines, and Canarian rum make excellent gifts. Hand-made cigars are popular, as are the numerous objects and utensils made from the local terracotta. Embroidery, open-work and threadwork in the form of tablecloths, linen and aprons make truly Canarian souvenirs, as do the island's beautiful flowers, straw-work and wood carvings.

INLAND FROM SANTA CRUZ

Inland from the capital is the ancient university town of **La Laguna**, set in spectacular countryside. **La Orotava**, within a valley on the north coast, is a beautiful example of old colonial architecture and has exceptional landscaped gardens.

Puerto de la Cruz, near La Orotava, lies on the northern shores and is an important tourist resort combining both traditional old charm and modern facilities. Near Icod, on the northwest coast, is the pretty village of **Garachico**, famous for the natural rock pools of **El Caletón** and **El Puertito** and a valuable silver cross which you'll see at **San Marcos** parish church. Heading south through rugged scenery on a tortuous route passing **Santiago de Teide**, the road rises towards the coast to present a panoramic view of the **Cliffs of the Giants**. There is something in Tenerife for all visitors, from stunning expanses of black or golden sand, to the dramatic mountain scenery or the peaceful town plazas and picturesque old buildings.

La Laguna ★★

Just inland from Santa Cruz, in a beautiful valley, is the island's second most important town, **La Laguna**. Founded in 1496 by Alonso Fernández de Lugo, this is a university town, with an important 16th-century neo-Classical cathedral and the Church of **Nuestra Señora de la Concepción**. To the west of the town is the popular seaside resort of **El Arenal**. Nearby is **Los Rodeos** airport.

The **Santa Iglesia Cathedral** houses a vast Baroque altarpiece, La Virgin de los Remedios, a silver altar, fine Flemish works of art, an English organ, and a 1767 marble pulpit. The 16th-century Church of Nuestra Señora de la Concepción has a fine Mudéjar carved wooden ceiling and an exceptional Baroque wooden pulpit from the 18th century. Said to be the island's most beautiful church, it has a six-tiered tower and three naves.

Until 1723, Laguna was the island's capital. Laguna boasts a string of fine religious buildings such as the 17th-century **Bishop's Palace**, monasteries, hermitages, convents (such as those of San Francisco and Santa Catalina) and palaces like **La Nava**, and its huge ancient dragon tree, located in the Seminary Gardens.

Around the north coast of the island is the site of the defeat of the native Guanches by the Spanish in 1494. The pretty village of **El Sauzal**, the **Playa del Roque**, the **Bajamar** clifftop resort and the **Hidalgo Point** are also interesting places to visit. To the north of Santa Cruz there are several sights surrounding the **Anaga mountain range** which rises up to 1000m (3281ft).

Below: *A storm rages over Puerto de la Cruz, a resort that has preserved its colonial grandeur.*
Opposite: *The city museums, art galleries and exhibition halls of Santa Cruz are housed in ornate buildings.*

Las Mercedes **

A steep, gullied sierra conceals the beautiful Las Mercedes forest, a botanist's paradise and packed with fascinating flora. The dense forests and jagged mountain scenery are best viewed from the **Pico del Inglés** mirador. On a clear day there's a breathtaking panorama of rugged peaks, rolling hills and the crystal-clear water of the Atlantic ocean to the north.

Northeast of the mirador, **Taganana** is a picturesque little village on the coast with good beaches nearby. Down the other side of the Anaga mountain chain is the fishing village of **San Andrés**, with its golden sand beach of **Las Teresitas**, just 5km (3 miles) north of the capital. Las Teresitas is a lovely artificial beach that is virtually deserted out of high season.

Tacoronte *

Tacoronte is famous for its wine and you can sample a glass or two in a local *bodega* (wine cellar). The highlight of this market town is the old Augustinian monastry, whose chapel houses the 17th-century **Cristo de los Dolores**, a statue modelled on an engraving by the great German Renaissance artist Albrecht Dürer, which is well worth seeing.

Below: *In 1975, four million sacks of Saharan sand were transported to Las Teresitas to create this beach north of Santa Cruz.*

La Orotava ***

Probably one of the prettiest towns on Tenerife, **La Orotava** is an architectural jewel, with many magnificent historic buildings and some cobbled streets. It's an old town but very well preserved.

Among Orotava's many interesting sites are the 18th-century Baroque **La Concepción Church**. It has a beautiful carved ceiling, as well as images and paintings from the 16th century. Other sites worth seeing include **San Juan** and the **Hermitage of El Calvario**.

Don't miss the **Museo de Artesania Ibero-Americana** within **Santo Domingo Convent** (la Casa de los Balcones), a masterpiece of traditional woodworking skills dating from 1632. Further up the hill, opposite the 18th-century **Hospital de la Trinidad**, there is a beautiful park and a 17th-century mill. You will see the most spectacular views of Puerto de la Cruz from Humboldt's viewpoint at La Cuesta de la Villa, on the outskirts of La Orotava.

Botanical Gardens of Acclimatization ★★
Take the road west from La Orotava to Puerto de la Cruz until you reach the 1788 Botanical Gardens of Acclimatization. The aim of this garden was to acclimatize plants and trees to the Canarian climate and then move them to the Spanish mainland. There is an astonishing variety of beautiful plants, trees and shrubs from all over the world. Open 09:00–19:00 April–September, 09:00–18:00 October–March, closed Good Friday, 25 December and New Year. Tel: (928) 38 35 72.

Puerto de la Cruz ★★
One of the top resorts in the Canary Islands, Puerto de la Cruz is a lively, atmospheric town with a fascinating history. Known locally as 'Puerto', its early prosperity

Above: *Over 4000 species of plant in Puerto de la Cruz's Botanical Gardens originated in Africa, Asia and America.*

FUN AND GAMES

Children will love **Loro Parque**, home to hundreds of brightly coloured parrots and friendly dolphins. It's just on the outskirts of Puerto de la Cruz and there are regular live shows to be enjoyed. Also great for children is **Zoolandia** on the eastern outskirts of Puerto – an interesting and humane zoo.

Adults should stop off at the **Bananera el Guanche**, off the Orotava road, a working plantation that gives a fascinating insight into how bananas are cultivated. More hedonistic thrill-seekers can head for Puerto's **casino** in the town itself and try their luck at the gaming wheels.

was based on the export of sugar and wine; later, cochineal and bananas. More recently, Puerto has been welcoming tourists, ever since the **Grand Hotel** was opened far back in 1886.

The main square, **Plaza Charco**, is the focal point for visitors and locals alike, who relax in the numerous bars and restaurants. There's a lovely old town just off the Plaza Charco around the fishing port, **Puerto Pesquero**, which is full of narrow, cobbled streets packed with imposing colonial architecture.

Above: *Magnificent Mount Teide, often covered in snow is the highest point in all Spanish territory.*

SPAIN'S HIGHEST PEAK

The **Caldera**, or Cauldron, of Teide, was formed 300,000 years ago, and the peak of **Mount Teide** pushed up 3718m (12,198ft) through the earth's crust in around 200,000BC. The National Park of Teide was created in 1954. Many rare plants and bird species are found in this natural wonderland. A cable car takes visitors up almost to the crater's rim to see Teide's Peak, which is snow-covered in winter. Strict regulations prevent the removal of plants or rocks from the park.

The National Park of Teide ★★★

Inland from La Orotava, take a trip into the **Cañadas del Teide** which dominates the island. From **El Portillo de Las Cañadas** (the Gateway) where there is a park and Visitor's Centre, a route runs east across the wonderful **La Esperanza Forest**, and the first mountain reached on this route, after Aguamansa, **Monte Verde** (Green Mountain), is aptly named as it is a botanical paradise. At **Las Raíces**, in a clearing in La Esperanza Forest, an obelisk commemorates General Franco's secret meeting in June 1936, where he carefully planned his military coup. Visit the fabulous caves called the **Cueva del Hielo**, to the right of the path, in order to see the ice stalactites.

The focus of the national park is its vast crater, called the Caldera de las Cañadas. Mount Teide is no more than a large cone lying on the edge of this crater which is even more spectacular than Teide itself. Teide National Park can be approached from **La Esperanza** village, to the north, from La Orotava to the west and also from **Boca del Tauce** in the south.

THE COAST

Among the many places to explore along Tenerife's north coast are the quaint old towns of Icod de Los Viños and San Marcos, while on the east coast you will come across the fascinating historic town of Garachico.

Icod de Los Viños ★★★

One of Tenerife's oldest towns, Icod lies on the island's north coast. Although it was founded by the Spanish in 1501, it was originally a Guanche settlement. Here is a famous dragon tree, said to be 1000 years old although the real age of this tree remains unknown. There are numerous religious monuments and churches, such as the convent of **San Agustín** and the beautiful Renaissance church of **San Marcos** on El Pilar Square.

San Marcos ★

The nearby village of San Marcos is small and quiet and a good place to get away from the crowds for a short while.Originally a fishing port, San Marcos is now becoming a popular resort, largely due to its beautiful beaches, excellent fish restaurants and lively bars.

Garachico ★★

Situated on Tenerife's northwestern shore, Garachico is a historic town which escaped the fury of Mount Teide's eruption in 1706. The town is filled with notable

---

LAND OF MIRADORS

One of the best views of Mount Teide is from the **Mirador Margarita Diedra**, on the road out of Orotava. The **Valley of Ariba Mirador** also offers stunning views of the mountain up through the **Ariba Valley**. The road up to the peak from La Laguna has many miradors, the **Pico de la Flores**, **El Diablillo**, the **Mirador of Ortuno** and the **Mirador Ayosa**.

Below: *Tenerife is a botanists' paradise with carpets of flowers during springtime.*

Above: *Garachico has many fine buildings in the process of being restored.*

WATERSPORTS

Watersports dominate the Canary Islands, with windsurfing being the most popular. You can rent scuba-diving equipment, sailboards, boats and jet skis at the major resorts. Surfers ride the waves at **Playa de Martianez** on Tenerife and **Maspalomas** on Las Palmas. For swimming, most resort beaches are safe, but do be careful on all other beaches: there may be dangerous undertows.

---

old buildings which include the palace of the counts of Gomera, the 1575 **San Miguel Castle** and, the **Santa Ana Church**, which houses works by the Canarian sculptor, José Lujan Pérez, and the convent of **San Francisco**. Currently, many of the town's fine buildings are being carefully restored. Located on an arc of land at the bottom of a volcanic valley, the town faces the weirdly shaped **Roque de Garachico**. Natural rock pools, which have been formed by the lava, have been converted into bathing pools of crystal-clear sea water. The port here was once the island's main harbour for agricultural exports.

Moving around the coast to the west side of the island, **Puerto del Santiago** is well-known for the nearby **Cliffs of the Giants**. The town has a wide bay and a large yacht harbour, and is fast becoming an upmarket resort. Near **Playa de la Arena** there is a beach of black volcanic sand.

Playa de las Américas and Los Cristianos *

These adjacent resorts are the most popular places in Tenerife. Year-round sunshine and a wealth of watersports and boat trips act as a magnet for hundreds of thousands of happy holidaymakers. **Playa de las Américas** has been unashamedly developed for fun in the sun. You won't find much traditional Canarian – or Spanish – culture here but there's plenty of boisterous nightlife and you won't have to look hard to find an English-style pub or a plate of fish and chips. **Los Cristianos** was once a tiny fishing village and retains traces of its original charm, particularly around the old harbour. Families should head for **Aguapark Octopus** nearby to brave the thrilling waterslides.

Heading east, the **Costa del Silencio** shelters a few small resorts like **Las Galletas**, with its Amarilla Golf and Country Club. The east coast leading back to Santa Cruz is peppered with lovely sheltered beaches. **Candelaria**, a few kilometres before the capital, is a world-famous place of pilgrimage. The town is dominated by an impressive basilica that houses a statue of Tenerife's patron saint, Nuestra Señora de la Candelaria.

> **THE BLACK MADONNA**
>
> In 1826, the statue of the Black Madonna of Candelaria, Tenerife's patron saint, was carried out to sea, from where it is said to have originated, by a huge tidal wave, and replaced by a copy which stands in the impressively spired basilica. Thousands of pilgrims congregate in Candelaria each year on 14 and 15 August.

Below: *The Basilica of Candelaria is one of Tenerife's most important pilgrimage attractions, housing a copy of an original statue of the Virgin which dated from the 1300s.*

Tenerife at a Glance

Named Tenerife after the Guanche words for 'White Mountain', the Canaries' largest island's name celebrates the Teide Peak that dominates Tenerife. To the north, where the capital is located, the island is green and often overcast or cloudy. In the arid south, the weather is more often sunny and cloudless. The weather, on the whole, is usually pleasant wherever you are on Tenerife.

GETTING THERE

Most visitors arrive by air at **Reina Sofía International Airport**. The nearest airport to Santa Cruz is **Los Rodeos** domestic airport. There are a number of **ferry services** which depart from Cádiz.

GETTING AROUND

A good **motorway** runs around the island from Puerto de la Cruz in the north, through Santa Cruz, down the east coast and along the south to Los Cristianos. A secondary **road** connects Los Cristianos with Puerto de la Cruz around the west side of the island making a coastal circumnavigation of Tenerife possible. Most roads on this island are well-surfaced.

WHERE TO STAY

Santa Cruz
LUXURY
Mency, Calle José Naveiras 38; tel: (922) 27 67 00, fax: 28 00 17; exquisitely furnished in Louis Quatorze style.

MID-RANGE
Colón Rambla, Viera y Clavijo 49; tel: (922) 27 25 50, fax: 27 27 16; good situation, pool.

BUDGET
Taburiente, Dr. José Naveiras 24-A; tel: (922) 27 60 00, fax: 27 05 62; impressive range of facilities for a two-star rating.
Hotel Atlantico, Calle del Castillo 12; tel: (922) 24 63 75; central location.

Puerto de la Cruz
LUXURY
Melía Botánico, Calle RJ Yeoward; tel: (922) 38 14 00, fax: 38 15 04; beautiful gardens.

MID-RANGE
Melía Puerto de la Cruz, Villanueva del Prado; tel: (922) 38 40 11, fax: 38 65 59; excellent central location.
El Tope, Calzada de Martianez 2, tel: (922) 38 50 52, fax: 38 00 03; near beach and town.

BUDGET
Bambi, Lomito 15; tel: (922) 38 45 51, fax: 38 34 24; not far from the beach.

La Orotava
MID-RANGE
Hotel Victoria, Calle de H. Apolinar 8; tel: (922) 33 16 83; restored 15th-century mansion.

Playas de las Américas
LUXURY
Gran Hotel Playa de Duque; tel: (922) 71 00 00; 19th-century Canary village style.

Sol Elite Tenerife, Playas de las Américas; tel: (922) 79 10 62; fax: 79 39 20, near the beach.

MID-RANGE
Park Club Europe, Avenida Maritima; tel: (922) 79 26 90; fax: 79 33 52, beach nearby.

BUDGET
Oro Negro, tel: (922) 79 06 12; pool, near the beach.

Los Cristianos
LUXURY
Paradise Park, Oasis del Sur; tel: (922) 79 47 62, fax: 79 48 59; wonderful views.

MID-RANGE
Hotel Princesa Dacil, Camino Penetración; tel: (922) 75 30 30, fax: 79 06 58; three stars.

BUDGET
Andrea's, Avenida Valle Menendez, s/n D.P. 38650; tel: (922) 79 00 12, fax: 79 42 70; central, cozy, basic facilities.

Bajamar
MID-RANGE
Nautilus, Avda. de las Piscinas 2, Bajamar; tel: (922) 54 05 00.

Realejo Alto
LUXURY
Maritim, Calle Burgado 1, tel: (922) 34 20 12; fax: 34 21 09; inland but very good location.

MID-RANGE
Bahia Praque, La Longuera, tel: (922) 38 04 00; fax: 34 31 98; three-star hotel.

Tenerife at a Glance

WHERE TO EAT

Garachico
BUDGET
Il Giardino, Calle Esteban de Ponte 8; tel: (922) 83 02 45; old house in the village.

Las Canadas
LUXURY
Parador Nacional Las Canadas del Tiende; tel: (922) 38 64 15, fax: 38 64 15; built like a ski chalet with balconies. Good local food.

Santa Cruz
La Riviera, Rambla General Franco 155; tel: (922) 27 58 12; said to serve the best food on Tenerife.
El Coto de Antonio, Calle General Goded 13; tel: (922) 27 21 05; wide variety of international cuisine.
La Estancia, Calle Mendez Nuñez 110; tel: (922) 27 20 49; local specialities.

La Orotava
Restaurante Sabor Canario, Calle del Escultor Estévenez 17; imaginative local dishes.

Playas de las Américas
Bistro, Edificio Vina del Mar; tel: (922) 79 07 18; good, inexpensive cuisine.
Borinquen Tropic, Edificio Borinquen; tel: (922) 79 00 08; typical local dishes.

Puerto de la Cruz
Marquesa, Quintana, fax: (922) 38 69 50; good fare on balcony overlooking square.

Castillo San Felipe, Avenida Luis Lavaggi; tel: (922) 38 21 13; international and local dishes.
Bodega La Muralla, Calle La Holla 40; tel: (922) 38 23 01; exquisite *tapas* and small economically priced dishes.

Los Cristianos
El Sol, Chez Jaques, Calle El Cabezo; tel: (922) 70 05 69; French flavour to local dishes.
El Rancho de Don Antonio, Calle Juan XXIII; tel: (922) 79 00 92; good steak dishes.

TOURS AND EXCURSIONS

Ceramic Museum, Puerto de la Cruz; open 10:00–18:00, Sundays 10:00–13:00.
Archaeological Museum, tel: (922) 20 93 17;
Anthropology Museum, tel: (922) 20 93 20; both open 10:00–20:00,Tuesday–Sunday.
Museo Municipal de Bellas Artes, open 10:00–20:00 Monday–Saturday.
Botanical Gardens of Acclimatization, Puerto de la Cruz; tel: (922) 38 35 72. Open 09:00–18:00; closed on Good Friday, 25 December and New Year.
Parrot Park, Puerto de la Cruz, open 08:30–17:00 daily; tel: (922) 37 40 81.

Bananera El Guanche, La Orotava; tel: (922) 33 18 53, open 08:30–13:00 and 14:00–18:30 daily.
Eagles of Teide Park, Los Cristianos, Arona, open 09:00–18:00.
Medieval Night, San Miguel Castle, tel: (922) 70 02 76, open 20:00 till late.
Canelo Centre, El Tanque, tel: (922) 13 33 93, open 10:00–18:00.
La Rosaleda Rose Park, Puerto de la Cruz, open 09:00–13:00.
Yellow Submarine, Las Galletas, tel: (922) 71 50 80, open 14:00–17:00.
Cabildo Insular de Tenerife, Palacio Insular, Plaza España, Santa Cruz, tel: (922) 60 55 00/92.

USEFUL CONTACTS

Tourist Information Centre, Plaza de la Iglesia, Puerto de la Cruz, tel: (922) 38 60 00; www. puertocruzturismo.org
Airports: Los Rodeos (North), tel: (922) 25 77 45 or 63 58 00; for bookings, tel: (922) 25 23 40. Iberia, tel: 77 13 75. **Reina Sofía** (South), tel: (922) 77 00 54. Iberia, tel: 77 13 75.
Gomera Ferry, Los Cristianos, tel: (922) 97 02 15.

WEST CANARY ISLANDS	J	F	M	A	M	J	J	A	S	O	N	D
AVERAGE TEMP. °C	18	18	19	19	21	22	25	25	24	23	21	19
AVERAGE TEMP. °F	64	64	66	66	70	72	77	77	75	73	70	66
HOURS OF SUN DAILY	6	7	7	8	9	10	11	10	8	7	6	6
DAYS OF RAINFALL	7	6	5	4	2	1	1	1	2	6	10	9
RAINFALL mm	36	8	2	11	2	0	0	0	6	3	58	9
RAINFALL in	1.5	0	0	0.5	0	0	0	0	0	0	2	0

7
La Palma

With possibly the most beautiful mountain scenery in the whole of the Canary Islands, and known as 'La Isla Bonita' (the pretty island), La Palma is peaceful and unspoilt. In relation to its total area, it is one of the steepest islands in the world. Almond trees cloak La Palma with clouds of scented blossom in springtime and banana plantations cling precariously to its steep slopes.

The island itself is pear-shaped, with a rocky coast and a few good beaches. Although mostly green and fertile, the northern part of La Palma is dominated by the craggy **Roque de los Muchachos**, 2426m (7959ft) high. This looms over the **Caldera de Taburiente**, one of the world's largest volcanic craters, which is now a spectacular national park. The whole island is actually ideal for hiking and there's a wonderful variety of scenery to explore.

Santa Cruz is the capital of La Palma, a small, atmospheric city whose historic buildings help it to maintain its colonial charm, complemented by lively cafés and good restaurants. The wealth that was made from the days when the island was heavily involved in trade with the Americas is reflected in these grand old buildings. Also dotted around the island are numerous picturesque villages such as **San Andrés** and **Los Llanos de Aridane**. Most visitors to the island come to enjoy its natural beauty, but sun-lovers will find several good beaches, particularly the fine black sands of **Puerto de Naos** and **Puerto de Tazacorte** on the southwest coast.

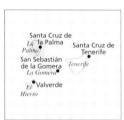

Don't Miss

*** La Cumbrecita: viewpoint overlooking the Caldera de Taburiente.
*** Santa Cruz: wonderful natural beauty and beaches.
** International Astrophysical Observatory: finest window on universe.
** Bosque de Los Tilos: UNESCO-protected forest.
** Fuencaliente: the island's southernmost point with two volcano cones.
** Puerto de Naos: with its fine black sand, the island's best beach.

Opposite: *The elegant old colonial port of Santa Cruz de la Palma edges the large harbour and yacht basin.*

POLICE

There are three types of police on the islands: the **Policía Municipal,** who are dressed in blue and direct traffic; the **Policía Nacional,** in brown, who look after urban areas and tourist trouble; and the **Guardia Civil,** in green, who look after the rural areas and everything else. Spanish police have a reputation for being rather uncooperative and trigger-happy but as long as you stay on the right side of the law there's no reason why you should have any trouble.

SANTA CRUZ DE LA PALMA

This important port is built in an amphitheatre shape overlooking the sea on the slopes of **La Caldereta** volcanic crater. It is located on the eastern side of the heart-shaped island, about halfway down the coastline. The main part of the city, founded in 1493, is clustered around the large harbour and yacht basin which is edged by a corniche known as the **Avenida Marítima**. Almost 20,000 people inhabit this pretty, restful city of whitewashed buildings and red-tiled roofs, which cascade down the steep hillsides along winding, narrow streets.

Santa Cruz de la Palma has not, in fact, really suffered a 'sea change' with the advent of tourism like many of the capitals of other Canarian islands. Not being the main port of entry to the island, it has retained its old-world colonial grace and elegance, unspoilt by shops and high-rise hotels.

The tall building dominating the harbour is the island government's council building, the **Cabildo Insular**. One main road, the Avenida Marítima, runs south to north through the city. It sports some of the most elegant Canarian architecture on the island, its beautiful old buildings, with typical one- and two-storied balconies, have intricate wooden railings and ornate carved panels embellished with family coats-of-arms. These face the sea front and their wooden balconies are echoed in the island's **National Parador** hotel.

Further north is the 16th-century **Castillo de Santa Catalina** which defended the city against the pirates, after the repulse of an attack by Francis Drake in 1595. It is open only on special occasions.

Just past the Naval Centre is a replica in concrete of Columbus's flagship, the *Santa María*. Columbus never actually visited La Palma, but this replica is used as a maritime museum which is known locally as the **Barco de la Virgen**. Open 09:30–14:00 Monday–Friday (summer), also 16:00–19:00 (winter), closed Saturday and Sunday.

Santa Cruz city has a wonderful **Museum of Natural History and Ethnology.** It is one of the best in the Canaries, and contains a wealth of information on the islands' fauna and flora, as well as housing a number of interesting zoological examples from the island's interior. The museum is housed in a restored 16th-century convent.

Next door to the museum is the **Fine Arts Gallery**, which has an interesting collection of Spanish and Flemish paintings. Open 09:00–14:00 and 16:00–18:30, daily.

Back in the city centre, the main shopping thoroughfare is known as **Calle O'Daly**, after an Irish businessman. Numerous small shops, cafés and restaurants line the street, interspersed with some fine, old, typically Canarian houses, built around shady court-yards which can be glimpsed through the wide doorways.

Above: *Traditional white-washed and modern buildings line Santa Cruz de La Palma's steep and narrow streets.*

MUSEUMS AND CHURCHES

Most museums and churches are closed to the public during festivals and on Sundays. Many churches post the times of their religious services on the door or gateway: visitors should respect these times when sightseeing and make sure they are properly dressed – no micro skirts, exposed shoulders or shorts. Sometimes it is necessary to find a museum curator to open a monument or historic building. Many houses on the islands which are architecturally important are often privately owned and therefore not open to the public.

San Salvador Church ★★

The city centre proper is the **Plaza de España**,
bordered by the Renaissance-style parish church of **San
Salvador**, the tall bell tower of which dominates the
square. The church has a fine Mudéjar coffered wooden
ceiling, and the altarpiece is a depiction of the
Transfiguration by the 19th-century artist Antonio Maria
Esquivel. The sacristy contains some fine Gothic wood-
work and the church's altar is also exquisitely carved.
The statue outside the **Real Convento** (Royal Convent)
of the Immaculate Conception is that of Felipe II, from
whose reign the building dates.

The stone fountain, in Plaza de España which is rather
impressive but non-functioning, dates from 1776, and the
nearby **Cabañas Palace**, which is open during office
hours, is a delightful example of contemporary wood
and stone architecture.

Town Hall ★★

The grand colonades to one side of the plaza are those of
the historic Town Hall (*Ayuntamiento*) which is also open
during office hours. Dating from the 16th century, this
was once the Cardinal's palace and inside are murals by
Mariano de Cossio as well as lovely, dark Canarian wood
panelling. Outside, the four columns of the Town Hall's
façade support a typically fenestrated upper floor, decorated with a plaque of Felipe II of Spain, the La Palma
coat of arms and those
of the Austrian Royal
Household. This triangular
'square' which is made up
of the Plaza de España and
the Calle O' Dally, is the
centre of city life in Santa
Cruz. For a relaxing coffee,
try the **Café La Placeta**,
in the small square of
Avenida Pérez de Brito.
The **Salazar Palace** is just a
short walk south.

**Santa Cruz
de La Palma**

1. Nuestra Senora de la Luz Hermitage
2. Plaza de Santo Domingo
3. Salazar Palace
4. Circo de Marte Theatre
5. San Sebastian Hermitage
6. San Salvador Church
7. Plaza de España
8. Town Hall
9. Parador (Hotel)
10. Chico Theatre
11. Market
12. Hospital
13. Our Lady of Dolores Church
14. Old Balconies
15. Hospital
16. San Jose Hermitage
17. San Francisco Plaza
18. San Francisco Convent
19. Santa Catalina Castle
20. Maritimo Hotel
21. Hotel
22. Hotel
23. Police Station
24. Church of the Incarnation
25. Museum of Nat. History

Tobacos Vargas *

For an interesting detour, visit the Tobacos Vargas on Avenida Maritima. Here you can see workers rolling the Palmero cigars by hand, and you'll be able to purchase some of the product which is said to rival those produced in Cuba. The cigar industry here was the result of regular migration between La Palma and Cuba.

TOURING THE ISLAND

Just outside Santa Cruz, to the north, is the 17th-century Sanctuary of the island's patron saint, **Nuestra Señora de Las Nieves** (Our Lady of the Snows), set in wooded mountain scenery.

Overshadowing the church, which contains an altar made of 18kg (40 lb) of Mexican silver, is the **Pico de Las Nieves,** a fine lookout. South from this is the **Mirador la Concepción,** with fine views of the city. The island's longest tunnel leads to the turn off for **La Cumbrecita** (Little Summit), part of the Cumbre mountain spine, which stands 1833m (6014ft) high. You'll see the vast crater rim of the **Caldera de Taburiente** from the lookout here, the nearby **Loma das Chozas** and the great spire of rock rising 800m (2625ft) from the crater floor known as **Idafe Rock**.

Above: *Gaily painted old colonial houses with wooden balconies in Santa Cruz.*

A TYPICAL TOWN HALL

The Casa Consistoriates, Ayuntamiento, or Town Hall, on Santa Cruz's Plaza de España, is one of the finest examples of its kind in the Canaries. It was built in typically ornate style during 1563.

The Coat of Arms of San Miguel de la Palma, the island's true name, is emblazoned on the front of the elegant building, which contains some exquisite wood carvings, frescos by Cossio, and some rare treasures dating from the 16th and 17th centuries. Be sure to see the extravagant staircase, the Banqueting Hall and the Mayor's Office.

MALMSEY WINE

This strong, full-flavoured
fortified white wine is known
as **Malvasia** or Malmsey,
after the grape it is made
from. It was made initially
only on **Tenerife**, and
became popular throughout
Europe and the Americas
between the 16th and
17th centuries, when it was
known as **Sack** (possibly
after the Spanish word *saca*
for exported goods). Much
of the Malvasia wine now
comes from **Lanzarote**,
particularly from the region
around **La Geria**. The largest
wine-producing area of the
Canaries is still northern
Tenerife. Muscatel is
another of the famous
Canarian wines, and a
unique wine made from
laurel berries on El Hierro
is known as *vino herreño*.

The main road now leads west to the island's second
largest settlement, **Los Llanos**. This is the market town
for the island's main agricultural region, specializing in
bananas, dates and almonds. Worth a visit is **Nuestra
Señora del Los Remedios**, a little 1517 church on Plaza
de España. Continuing west, through Argual, a detour
should be made to the **Mirador of Time** which is 594m
(1949ft) high. From the lookout on the island's most
picturesque valley, **Aridane**, you can see the spectacular
Gorge of Angustias. Returning to the main road, turn
down into **Tazacorte**, overlooking the shipping harbour
of Puerto de Tazacorte. Tazacorte was the site of the
murder of a Jesuit missionary, Fra Azevedo, who was
killed by pirates in 1570, and is commemorated in the
House of the Martyrs in the village. Puerto Tazacorte is
where the conquistador Alonso Fernández de Lugo
landed in 1492. From Puerto Tazacorte, take a boat trip
to the spectacular **Cueva Bonita**, a cave with eerie lighting
effects. Heading north, the town of **Tijarafe** is known for
its 16th-century altar in the **Church of Candeleria**. Just
before **Puntagorda**, there is a fine lookout for coastal
views. After **Briestas** village, a turning right leads up to a
mirador on the brooding, mist-shrouded **Roque de los
Muchachos**, the island's highest point.

Right: *Islanders celebrate
the festival of Nuestra
Señora de las Nieves, when
the jewelled statue of the
Virgin is carried from Las
Nieves to Santa Cruz.*
Opposite: *The National
Park of La Caldera de
Taburiente, caused by the
death of a volcano, is now
home to rare flora.*

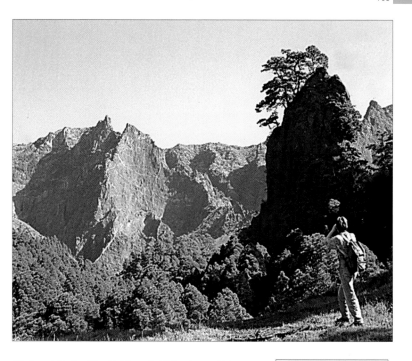

National Park of La Caldera de Taburiente ★★★

The gem at the heart of La Palma island is the National Park of La Caldera de Taburiente. The Caldera, or 'cauldron' is not, as many believe, a volcanic crater. About 400,000 years ago, the massive peak of an extinct volcano collapsed inward, creating one of the largest natural bowls in the world at 9km (5½ miles) in diameter. The 'death' of the volcano extinguished any further volcanic activity in the entire area. The earth-shattering collapse caused a dent in the rim extending to the southwest. This acted as an outlet for the two rivers which converged to form the **Rio de Las Angustias** which currently has its outflow near Puerto de Tazacorte on the island's west coast.

Declared a national park in 1954, this vast depression, dominating the northern half of La Palma, rises to its highest point, the **Roque de los Muchachos,** at 2426m

EXOTIC FRUITS

The Canary Islands have the perfect climate for growing a variety of fruits and exotic plants. Some plants are grown commercially such as tobacco from Cuba; bananas from Africa and India; sugar cane from India; and the Strelizia (Bird of Paradise) flower from South Africa. Others are grown more as a novelty. The Mexican *zapote* tree, from which chewing gum comes; cherimoya, (custard apple), papaya, pineapple and avocado all come from Central America. The peri-melon comes from Peru, as well as kiwi and passion fruit.

Above: *The world-famous International Astrophysical Observatory is home to Europe's largest telescope.*

(7959ft). On the road to the peak you will pass the **International Astrophysical Observatory** which was opened in 1985. The observatory is situated on La Palma for a reason: its geographical location and the excellent climatic conditions do not interfere with astrophysical observations. The clear air and cloudless nights were found to be ideal for astronomy, and the Swedes even built a special 'sun tower' here housing instruments used in observing the sun. The main building houses Europe's largest telescope. It is one of the most important observatories in the world, and several countries contributed to its foundation. The Observatory Roque de los Muchachos is reached by a new track from Miranda (visits only by arrangement).

The remoteness of the island and its lack of development means that the observatory is free from distracting artificial light. The shape of the mountain and the prevailing winds also means that the airflow remains undisturbed. From January to March snow lies on the crater rim and it can be cold at these heights. The observatory is situated quite high up, above the clouds for most of the year. This is rather convenient as clouds trap dust and moisture whch interferes with the airflow.

As one of the most important parks in Spain, not only for its spectacular scenery but because of its precious and unique flora, the Caldera is managed by ICONA, the national forestry agency. ICONA, together with the UNESCO biosphere programme, is also responsible for La Palma's other unique natural feature, the **Los Tilos** forest in the northeast of the island which contains many of the lovely 'laurisilva' trees. In each site, the organizations have an information and ecological research centre.

The information centre of the **Caldera de Taburiente** is located at the end of the road which gives the easiest access to the Caldera. From near the town of El Paso, off the Santa Cruz de La Palma to Los Llanos road, a side road leads up to an interesting lookout known as **La Cumbrecita**. Nearby are two magnificent sites from which one can view the vast crater.

Both the **Mirador los Roques** and the **Mirador las Chozas** give the visitor some of the best views across the deep crater. Directly in front of the lookouts is an interesting rock pinnacle known as the **Roque de Idafe**. This spire was once worshipped by Guanche natives in pre-Columbian times and was the site of human sacrifices. Right across the other side of the crater, you'll be able to see the sharp outline of the Roques de los Muchachos and if the weather is clear you can make out the dome of the Observatory perched on the crater rim.

INSECT-COLOURED SILK

The small village of El Paso, near the road to La Cumbrecita, is renowned for its handmade silk, the only place in Spain where it is produced traditionally. A natural dye was first used in the 18th century to colour the silk. This was extracted from a lichen called *orchillo*, found on coastal rocks. In the early 19th century, a bug, which lives on the *optunia* (prickly pear), was introduced. When crushed, the bug produced a deep carmine dye, which was employed to colour the natural silk. Almond shells, when processed, were also used to give the silk a beige hue. In El Paso today, these three natural dyes are still used to produce vividly coloured silk items snapped up as souvenirs by tourists.

Below: *Breathtaking view from the Roque de los Muchachos into the Taburiente crater.*

Inside the huge crater is a wonderful fertile valley packed with colourful and unusual shrubs, trees and flowers, aided by frequent rain and damp, cool clouds. At certain heights, various types of vegetation thrive. From 1300m (4265ft) an unusual type of tree heather, *Erica arborea,* and the faya tree (*Myrica faya*) exist side by side. The faya is culled by locals as it is ideally suited for use as props for banana plants, grown on the terraces in the west of the island. From 1000m (3300ft) the **Canary Pine forest** extends up to almost 2000m (6200ft). This pine is unusual because it has the ability to withstand the forest fires which occasionally rage through La Palma's wooded areas. Unique to the Canaries is the 4m (13ft) high, biennial pininana flower. This unusual plant blooms blue on La Palma and red on Tenerife. La Palma violets also thrive in the caldera, as does the yellow-flowered cordeso and the pink and white cistus. Laurisilva, another of the Canarys' rare species of tree, which is not a real laurel, also proliferates at a certain level on the crater rim's slopes.

THE DRAGON TREE

Dracaena draco, the dragon tree, sprouts like a giant mushroom in gardens and in the wilds of most of the Canary Islands. Said to be descended from a prehistoric type of vegetation, this strange tree, with its gnarled trunk and spiky, clustered leaves, certainly grows to a very old age, but its lack of rings means that it is impossible to date accurately. In ancient times, the Guanches used the resin as an ingredient for embalming their chiefs. They also used it to dye their garments. Dragon trees are now protected by government decree, and there are many fine specimens throughout the islands.

Returning to the island's north road, turn right and take a detour to the clifftop village of **Santa Domingo de Garafia** for views of the rocky coast and to see the fine church. There is a secret fountain near the crossroads at **Llano Negro** and the **Cueva de la Zarza** is the site of many Guanche rock inscriptions.

Passing the turning left to **Franceses**, to the right of the main road is **Roque Faro**, a goat-rearing centre. After **Barlovento** village, the road heads down to the junction with a road leading to the **Punta Cumplida** lighthouse, with fine coast vistas. Continue on the main road to **Los Sauces**, site of the 16th-century **Nuestra Señora de Monserrat** church which contains a 17th-century statue of the Virgin and a Flemish-style altarpiece. If you make a detour to the coastal village of **San Andrés y Sauces**, near the Barranco de Agua, you'll come across the picturesque fishing port of **Espindola**. Also near San Andrés is **El Charco Azul**, the Blue Pool.

Bosque de los Tilos ★★★

The main road leads through deep gorges and, before the Barranco Galga lookout at San Bartolomé, the **Bosque de los Tilos**, a UNESCO-protected forest, is beautiful and well worth a visit. Halfway between here and Santa Cruz is the pretty town of **Puntallana**.

The south of the island vies with the north for natural beauty and the road which should be taken out of Santa Cruz leads up past the **Mirador El Risco**, or **Mirador de la Concepción**, through to Brena Alta which is famous for its palm weaving. There is a tobacco factory where you can buy good samples as souvenirs, and then you will pass two impressive dragon trees, and make you way down to **Breña Baja**. The International Airport is located south of here. Take the main, coastal road and look for the **Cueva de Belmaco** with its Guanche rock inscriptions.

> **MIRADORS ON THE ISLAND**
>
> - **Pico de las Nieves:** 2247m (7372ft).
> - **Panorama La Cumbrecita:** 1633m (5357ft).
> - **Vulcán de San Antonio:** 657m (2155ft).
> - **Mirador El Time:** 594m (1948ft).
> - **Roque de los Muchachos:** 2426m (7959ft).

Mazo ★★

Take the top road to see the 16th-century statues of the Virgin in the church of **San Blas** in the charming village of Mazo. During the festival of Corpus Christi, from May to June, the villagers decorate Mazo with carpets of flowers and arches of greenery. The village is well-known for its pottery and it's worth paying a visit to **El Molino**, on the main road after Breña Baja, a craft school. You'll also be able to buy souvenirs like woven baskets and embroidered tablecloths from the workshop.

Continuing through the villages of Monte de Luna and Las Caletas, the main road enters **Fuencaliente**. Today the village is noted for its excellent Malvasia wine and almond biscuits. Nearby are two volcanoes: **San Antonio** and **Teneguia** (formed when San Antonio erupted in 1971).

Opposite: *Dragon trees are quite common in the wilds throughout the islands. Their blood-red sap was used in ancient Guanche rituals.*

Below: *Appreciate the natural beauty of Las Palma's extinct volcanoes by exploring on foot.*

Near the San Antonio volcano is the spectacular **Roque Teneguia**, a spire once revered by the native Guanches. The Teneguia volcano is particularly interesting as it has only recently erupted. You'll discover that the ground is still warm under your feet. Also, the views from here of the wild lava landscape are spectacular. From this lookout you can walk down to the two lighthouses on the rocky **Punta de Fuencaliente**. After visiting the two volcanoes, take a detour west off the main road to **Las Indias** on the coast for stunning views of the bays. Back on the route north, past **El Charco**, is **Las Manchas**, where you'll see the fine, black sand beach of Puerto de Naos.

Puerto de Naos ★★★

The beach can only be reached by driving north through **Los Llanos** and back down to the steep coast, clad with banana plantations. Puerto de Naos is the best beach on La Palma and is the west coast's largest resort, located 11km (7 miles) south of Tazacorte.

The road winds through **San Nicolas**, a village split in two because of the volcanic eruption of Nambroque, in 1949, which left the little church isolated among the lava fields. As you approach Los Llanos, you will drive through **Tajuya** village, around which the region becomes highly agricultural with fruit and almond orchards, profuse flower gardens and tobacco plantations.

Right: *The black sand beach of Puerto de Naos.*

La Palma at a Glance

Best Times to Visit

Temperatures vary little on La Palma throughout the year, but there is plenty of rain from November to the end of March. The sea temperatures are consistant and one can swim all year round.

Getting There

Most visitors from abroad, apart from those from the Spanish mainland, arrive by air at **La Palma International Airport**. There are **ferry services** from Cádiz for passengers and cars to Santa Cruz.

Getting Around

La Palma has a good bus service but most people prefer to travel off the bus routes. This is why **car hire** is the best way to get around. Prices vary but mileage is usually unlimited. Organized **coach tours** take visitors to various island attractions. Coach excursions can be joined from pre-arranged pick-up points and can last for a half or full day.

Where to Stay

Santa Cruz
Luxury
Parador Nacional Santa Cruz, Avenida Maritima 34; tel: (922) 41 23 40, fax: 41 18 56; prestigious hotel in villa.

Mid-range
Hotel Maritimo, Avda. Maritimo 80; tel: (922) 42 02 22, fax: 41 43 02; good position on harbour.

Brena Baja
Mid-range
Hacienda San Jorge, Playa de los Cancajos; tel: (922) 18 10 66, fax: 43 45 28; Spanish-style hotel near small beach.

El Paso
Budget
Nambroque, Calle Montelujan; tel: (922) 48 52 79; well-located, great facilities.

Fuencaliente
Budget
Apartamentos Colón, Los Quemados; tel: (922) 44 41 55; views of vineyards and the sea.

Where to Eat

Santa Cruz
Chipi Chipi, Juan Mayor 42; tel: (922) 41 10 24; excellent dishes with typical hot sauces. Closed Wednesday, Sunday.

El Paso
La Cascada, Carretera de la Cumbre; tel: (922) 48 57 27; good pork dishes with *gofio*.

Fuencaliente
Parrilla Junonia, Los Canarios, Carretera General 49; tel: (922) 44 40 21; fresh fish and meat.

Breña Baja
Casa Pancho, La Polvacera 283; tel: (922) 43 48 34; fresh fish, pork and rabbit dishes.

San Andrés y Sauces
Meson del Mar, Puerto Esindola; tel: (922) 45 03 05; best fish restaurant.

Tours and Excursions

Botanical Excursions: Avenida del Puente 18, No. 3B, Santa Cruz de La Palma; tel: (922) 41 55 32.
Visits to the Astrophysical Observatory (Roque de los Muchachos): Instituto de Astrofisica de Canarias; tel: (922) 40 55 00 or 41 15 52.
Sportsfishing Club: la Gaviota, Avenida del Puente 27, No 1 Santa Cruz; tel: (922) 42 02 41.
Mountaineering: Los Llanos de Aridane; tel: (922) 46 00 85.

Useful Contacts

Aeropuerto de la Palma, tel: (922) 44 61 00 or 41 15 40.
IBERIA Airlines,Real 30, Santa Cruz, tel: (922) 41 31 60.
Tourist Information Offices
Santa Cruz: Paseo Maratimo/ Calle O'Daly, tel: (922) 41 19 57 or 41 21 06.
Puerto de la Cruz: Tourist Information Office, Plaza de la Iglesia 3, tel: (922) 38 60 00 or 37 02 43.
Travel Agents
Bandama: Avenida Maritima 20, Santa Cruz; tel: (922) 41 50 57, fax: 41 50 57.
Viajes Calima: Apuran 9, Santa Cruz; tel: (922) 42 00 04.
Viajes Insular: Plaza de España 2, Santa Cruz; tel: (922) 46 04 59.
Palmatur: Alvarez de Abreu 72, Santa Cruz; tel: (922) 42 04 94.
Omnibus service: tel: (922) 41 19 24 or 46 02 41.
Ferry service: Transmediterranea, tel: (922) 41 11 21.

8
La Gomera and El Hierro

Almost circular in shape, with the **National Park of Garajonay** in its centre, **La Gomera** is an extinct volcano and is thoroughly unspoilt. Once inhabited by a proud branch of the Guanche race, this sixth largest island of the Canary archipelago is still comparatively wild, ringed by steep cliffs, crammed with high peaks and covered by lush foliage. About two-thirds of the 372km² (144 sq mile) island is forested, and it is dominated by the massif of **Garajonay**, rising to 1487m (4879ft), whose jagged spines radiate out towards the sea. There are six major *barrancos* (gorges) dividing the countryside.

An important natural feature is the vast cedar forest, the **Bosque del Cerdo**, not far from the capital, and mastic gum trees, pines, and moss-encrusted silver laurel abound in the numerous deep valleys, dating back millions of years. The forests of La Gomera have been declared a Natural Heritage of Mankind site by UNESCO, and are criss-crossed with tracks which are ideal for walkers.

El Hierro is the smallest and least known of all the Islands. Visitors who seek peace and quiet are drawn to this westerly island which offers wonderful walking opportunities. Superb pine forests, sheer mountain walls and fantastic lookout points or *miradores* are also available to the visitor. A great natural feature of El Hierro is the bay of **El Golfo** (the Gulf). Some believe this to be the rim of a large crater, half of which is sunken and the other rising theatrically to over 1000m (3281ft).

Santa Cruz de
La la Palma
Palma   Santa Cruz de
          Tenerife
San Sebastián
de la Gomera   *Tenerife*
La Gomera
   El • Valverde
Hierro

DON'T MISS

*** Playa de Santiago: stony beach overlooked by quaint fishing village.
*** Valle Gran Rey: called 'Valley of the Great King' with beautiful views of the valley. Enjoy the emerald-green slopes, pretty villages and La Playa Calera.
*** Parque Nacional de Garajonay: contains a woodland of ferns, laurels and heath trees. This *Laurasilva* forest offers popular walks.
*** Vallehermoso: features the spectacular Los Organos rock formations.
*** Hermigua: the island's richest banana-growing area.

Opposite: *Gomeran farmers plant crops on steep hillsides terraces.*

SIGHTS TO SEE

*** Christopher Columbus's House: the explorer's base on the island.
*** Torre de Conde: Pre-Columbian Americana Museum.
*** Pozzo de Aguada: well from which the expeditions drew their last water before sailing to the New World.
*** Church of The Assumption: links to Columbus and the Conquistador Cortez.

Right: *The dense forest of the Garajonay National Park dominates La Gomera and is a favourite spot for hiking.*

LA GOMERA

This island is often shrouded in cloud, and can only be reached by a 90-minute ferry trip or half-hour hydrofoil from **Los Cristianos** in Tenerife, as there is no commercial airport on the island. This isolation, and the lack of golden sandy beaches, keeps many would-be holidaymakers at arm's length. Visitors come here mainly for the fantastic and dramatic scenery and for its tranquil, laid-back atmosphere and way of life. Just under 18,000 people live here, many of whom show the typical features of their Guanche ancestors. Other Canarios are known to make jokes about the Gomerans and poke fun at the isolated islanders. Handfashioned pottery, dating from around

3000BC, has been found in the area of **Fortaleza** which is situated in the centre of the island. Similar pots, the ochre-coloured, beautifully glazed 'ollas', are still being made on the island today.

Above: *A typical Gomerian building at Hermigua, La Gomera.*

A Brief History

In the late 15th and early 16th centuries, **Christopher Columbus** and **Hernando Cortez** visited the island. This was Columbus's final port of call before his historic journey across the Atlantic in 1492. It's La Gomera's main claim to international fame. The island's other link with the New World is that many Gomerans emigrated to Venezuela. The tiny capital, **San Sebastián**, nestles in the folds of the sunny east coast, while the north coast receives a year-round buffeting from the rain-filled northeast trade winds. One main road rings the **National Park of Garajonay**, with spur roads or connections to the six major villages of Hermigua, Agulo, Vallehermoso, Valle Gran Rey, La Rajita and Playa de Santiago. The largest hotel, **Hotel Jardín Tecina**, is situated above Santiago beach and consists of a village of cabana-like, cliff-top bungalows.

Above: *The natural har-bour of San Sebastián, last port of call for Columbus before setting sail on his 1492 voyage of discovery.*

SAN SEBASTIAN DE LA GOMERA

A giant statue of Christ overlooks the island's capital. The statue's arm is outstretched towards the distant Americas. San Sebastián harbour is one of the finest natural harbours in the entire Canary Islands. Rather disappointing initially, a closer look at this town reveals some interesting architecture. Consisting mostly of box-like, whitewashed, modern buildings, this port has no high-rise structures but does have a few pretty, Spanish Baroque and Moorish-style, pantiled houses built around shady courtyards. The Town Council building contains works by a local painter, José Aguilar. The city's main square and meeting place is **Plaza Calvo Sotelo**.

Christopher Columbus

The house at number 56 **Calle del Medio** is where Columbus stayed in San Sebastián, and is now a museum. Nearby is the well-house he used, known as the **Pozzo de Aguada**, which bears the legend 'With this Water, America was Baptized'. Columbus's ships, the *Santa María*, *Nina* and *Pinta*, arrived in San Sebastián on the explorer's first voyage to discover the New World in

1492. The three ships set sail from La Gomera, the last land they would set foot on before their arrival in the Americas. The next time Columbus arrived in La Gomera he came with a fleet of 17 ships on his second voyage west in October 1493. Again, in 1498 and in 1502, Columbus used the port as his final replenishing point before venturing out across the Atlantic Ocean.

Church of the Assumption **

Between the well-house and the house where Columbus stayed is the 15th-century **Church of the Assumption**, where the explorer heard his last mass before departing on his epic voyage. The exterior doorway has a remarkable lava-stone, Gothic central façade, and frescoes, created in 1760, which depict a fleet of English ships on the attack. A plaque on the wall records the worship of the Spanish conquistador, Hernando Cortez, in this church.

Below: *Torre del Conde in San Sebastián is the oldest military building on the islands and was once home of Beatriz de Bobadilla, mistress of Columbus.*

Torre del Conde ***

Currently a National Historic Monument, this Torre del Conde or Count's Tower dates back to 1447. This ancient tower is the oldest surviving military building in the Canaries. The Torre del Conde also contains an important museum of fascinating pre-Columbian Americana, celebrating the connection of the island with the vast continent around 6500km (4000 miles) to the west.

The tower was built in 1447 and it's the town's

Above: *Los Organos, the spectacular basalt cliff near Vallehermoso, comprised hundreds of columns of rock.*

most striking monument. Beatriz de Bobadilla used it as a refuge after the slaying of her husband, Hernán Peraza in 1487. Today it is surrounded by a car park, with an odd palm tree standing out in relief.

EL HIERRO

This is the smallest of the Canary Islands, at only 277km² (106 sq miles). Approximately 7000 people live on El Hierro, which lies, like an inverted anvil, way out in the southwestern corner of the archipelago. This tranquil island is devoid of any form of commercialism and is packed with incredibly beautiful and rather dramatic scenery.

The people of El Hierro are the descendants of the ancient **Bimbache** tribes, who worshipped the sacred Garoe evergreen tree, which produced water from its leaves. In Roman times, the island was inhabited by giant lizards, a throwback to the prehistoric iguanas which once thrived here. In his *Natural History*, Pliny called Hierro, 'Lagartaria', or 'Land of the Lizards', and a few examples of these creatures exist to this day on the Roques de Salmor, off the northwest coast.

For thousands of years, until Columbus proved otherwise, El Hierro was considered the end of the world. The first zero meridian was originally measured from the old lighthouse on **Orchilla**, the island's westernmost tip. This was the last piece of land which

INTERESTING ALTERNATIVES

*** El Golfo: huge, crescent-shaped bay on the west coast, fantastic views.
** Frontera: the island's second settlement and famous wine region.
** Sabinosa: famous for spa spring waters; westernmost settlement.
** Pozo de la Salud: underwater fishing attraction.
** El Tamaduste: a natural pool of remarkably clear water
** Tinor: spectacular formations of volcanic ash amid bright green fields.

Columbus was to see until he landed in the Bahamas in 1492. Today, the main occupation on the island is cultivating the rich volcanic soil and raising cattle. Minor roads link several beauty spots and hamlets, as well as the island's Parador, one of only two hotels on El Hierro.

Below: *The ferry for El Hierro leaves from the picturesque village of Santiago on La Gomera.*

Below: *Herreño fishermen: fresh fish caught in the deep Atlantic Ocean are a staple ingredient of the Canarian diet.*

Valverde **

With exactly half of the island's inhabitants living in the capital, Valverde is a quiet, tranquil town with beautiful gardens, orchards, squares and a fine central plaza. The parish church is worth a visit, as are the town's market and fish restaurants. Unusually for the Canary Islands, this capital lies around 5km (3 miles) inland from the port of El Puerto de la Estaca, and a little less from the island's airport, both located on the east coast. The island's only state-run Parador is located at the end of a 14km (9 mile) coastal road which runs along the base of the sheer mountain wall of El Risco de los Herrenos, to the south of Valverde.

El Golfo ***

The large, 14km (9 mile) long, crescent-shaped bay of El Golfo in the west of the island was once part of a giant

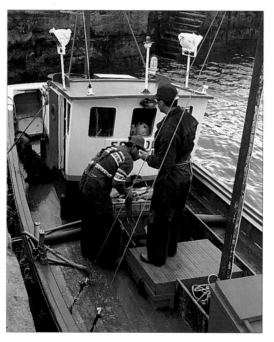

volcano rim, and it is the only place that the steep cliffs which surround the entire island, give way to a sloping shoreline. Its terraces, and El Golfo Valley, are ideal for growing paw paw, bananas, avocados, almonds, figs and vines.

This is the best point from which to see the bay. The high plateau in the centre of the island rises to 1501m (4295ft) at **Malpaso Point**. Volcanic craters dot the island's interior, a fertile area which supports trees that are hundreds of years old. **Frontera village,** almost in the centre of the island, is located in a good wine-producing region.

La Gomera and El Hierro at a Glance

BEST TIMES TO VISIT

The weather here is fine throughout the year. The northern side of the island, as well as the mountain forests can be quite damp. The islands of La Graciosa, Montaña Clara and Alegranza are generally hotter than El Hierro due to their close aspect to the African coast.

GETTING THERE

The best way to get to La Gomera is by **ferry** from Los Cristianos in the south of Tenerife to San Sebastián on La Gomera. Both a subsidiary of the Fred Olsen Line and Compania Transmediterranea run ferry services. El Hierro is reached from La Palma by **plane**. To get to the other smaller islands it's much easier to hire a **boat**.

GETTING AROUND

The **bus service** is less reliable on La Gomera than on the larger islands. A **hire car** is best to get around the island.

WHERE TO STAY

La Gomera
LUXURY
Parador Nacional Conde de La Gomera, San Sebastián; tel: (922) 87 11 00; good restaurant.

MID-RANGE
Garajonay, Calle Ruz de Padron 15, San Sebastián; tel: (922) 87 05 50; limited facilities, but central.

El Hierro
LUXURY
Parador del Hierro, Las Playas 26; tel: (922) 55 80 36, fax: 55 80 86; welcoming and well-furnished.

MID-RANGE
Boomerang, Calle Dr Gost 1, Valverde, El Hierro; tel: (922) 55 02 00, fax: 55 02 53; situated in town, friendly and comfortable.
Punta Grande Hotel, Las Puntas, Frontera, El Hierro; tel: (922) 55 90 81; quaintly listed as the smallest hotel in the world, classed as a two-star hotel it has marvellous views and a good restaurant.

BUDGET
Casanas, San Francisco 9; tel/fax: (922) 55 02 54; friendly and cheap.

WHERE TO EAT

La Gomera
Casa del Mar, Avenida Fred Olsen 61, San Sebastián, La Gomera; tel: (922) 87 12 19; fronting the beach with *pargo* fish and *ternera,* a speciality. Closed Sundays.
Mirador del Palmarejo, Carretera Gral. de Arure, 38870, Valle Gran Rey; La Gomera; tel: (922) 80 58 68; regional food is prepared by students of gastronomy.
La Romantica, Boulevard La Oliva, s/n; tel: (922) 80 07 41; roast chicken and pizza a speciality.

El Hierro
Casa Juan, Valverde, El Hierro; tel: (922) 55 80 02; tempting seafood, worth sampling.
Punta Grande Hotel, Las Puntas-Frantera, El Hierro; tel: (922) 55 90 81; fax: 55 90 81; four rooms, school restaurant. Closed Monday and Tuesday.

TOURS AND EXCURSIONS

The **C.I.T.** (Centro de Iniciatives y Tourismo del Norte de La Gomera) organize guided tours, tel and fax: (922) 14 41 01.
The Juego de Bolas Visitor's Centre of Garajonay National Park (UNESCO and ICONA) organize tours. Park Offices: San Sebastián, La Gomera; tel: (922) 80 09 93.
Los Organos: excursions by boat from Valle Gran Rey, Playa de Santiago and other ports on La Gomera.
El Golfo: best to visit the west side of this island.
El Pinar: in the centre of El Hierro, a forest of Canarian pines with numerous lookouts.

USEFUL CONTACTS

Tourist Board, Cabildo Insular del Hierro, Valverde; tel: (922) 14 01 47.
Patronado de Turismo, Licenciado Bueno 1, Valverde; tel: (922) 55 03 02.
Aeropuerto de Hierro Valverde; tel: (922) 44 01 15.
Tourist Information Office, Dr. Quintero 11, Valverde; tel: (922) 14 01 47.
Autos Cruz Alta Car Hire, Valverde, tel: (922) 55 03 49.

Travel Tips

Tourist Information

The **Spanish Tourist Office** maintains offices in France (Paris), Italy (Milan), Germany (Munich), America (New York), Australia (Sydney) and Canada (Toronto). The **Spanish Tourist Office** has its headquarters in London at 57-58 St James Street London SW 1A 1LD; tel: (171) 499 1169, fax: (171) 629 42 57.

Local Island Tourist Boards offer general advice, sell tickets, rent cars and offer trips and other services but may not speak much English. You will find them all over the islands and in the major resorts; the main ones are as follows:

Fuerteventura, Avenida 1st May 39, Puerto del Rosario. tel: (928) 85 14 00, fax: 85 18 12.

Lanzarote, Parque José Ramírez Cerda; tel/fax: (928) 81 18 60.

Tenerife, Cabildo Insular de Tenerife, Palacio Insular, Plaza de España, Santa Cruz; tel: (922) 24 22 27, fax:60 57 81.

La Palma, Calle O'Daly 22, Santa Cruz; tel: (922) 41 16 41 or 41 19 57 or 41 21 06.

La Gomera, Calle Medio 4, San Sebastian; tel: (922) 14 01 47 or 87 01 55 or 14 01 51.

El Hierro, Cabildo Insular del Hiero, Valverde; tel: (922) 55 03 02, fax: 55 10 52. Visit the Canary Islands website: www.gobcan.es

Entry Requirements

No visa is required, but visiters must have a valid passport. British, Australian, Canadian, New Zealand and American visitors can stay for up to three months. Those staying longer require visas, and workers need a special permit. If you lose your passport, contact the consul of the country of issue and they will advise you how to obtain the necessary documentation.

Customs

The Canary Islands are a **free-trade zone** and there are no restrictions on what you may bring with you as a tourist. The amount of wine, spirits, tobacco and other goods that can be taken in and out of the Canary Islands depends on whether you are travelling to or from an EU country, a non-EU country or a country outside Europe. Visitors should check in their country of residence before travelling abroad.

Health Requirements

No special vaccinations are required except for those visiting from endemic smallpox, cholera or yellow fever zones. **Typhoid** and **paratyphoid vaccinations** are recommended by British Health Authorities. Nationals of EU countries, including British visitors, can obtain a certain degree of free medical care with an **E111 form**, but medicines or dental treatment must be paid for. Take your E111 form to a local Instituto de la Seguridad Social (**Social Security Office**) when you have had medical treatment. Health insurance is recommended, and keep all receipts for treatment, in the event that you need to make a claim.

Getting There

By Air: There are regular cheap charter flights direct to Gran Canaria, Lanzarote, Fuerteventura and Tenerife from most western European cities. Scheduled flights are expensive and go via Madrid.

By Boat: Ferries from Cádiz on mainland Spain connect with Las Palmas on Gran

Canaria, Arrecife on Lanzarote and Santa Cruz on Tenerife. The ferry or hydrofoil from Los Cristianos on Tenerife runs to San Sebastián on Gomera.

What To Pack

The golden rule is to travel light whenever possible. There are several essentials to consider.

For women a shawl is useful because it can double up as a beach wrap, a head covering for church visits or as an evening wrap when a sudden drop in temperature could make you feel quite chilly. Men are advised to take a light jacket for the same reason. Dress as though you were in the tropics, with cotton shirts and trousers, light skirts or jeans, T-shirts, shorts (not recommended for church and business meetings), swimming costumes, a sarong and smart clothes for dining out. Take comfortable walking shoes, a pair of smarter shoes, at least one pair of sandals or 'flip-flops', sunglasses and a hat.

Should you forget something vital, local shops, especially those in resorts, sell most items of clothing ranging from the locally-made (which can be elegant and fashionable) to the designer labels. Canarians themselves usually dress casually.

Money Matters

Currency: The Spanish peseta (pta) is used throughout the islands and comes in notes of 1000, 2000, 5000 and 10,000ptas. Coins come in denominations of 5, 10, 25, 50, 100, 200 and 500ptas.

Currency exchange: You can change foreign currency or travellers' cheques at banks, post offices, bureaux de change and many hotels.

Banks: There are numerous banks throughout the islands, open on weekdays from 09:00–14:00 and Saturdays from 09:00–13:00. Banks will exchange Eurocheques free but will usually charge for exchanging travellers' cheques or currency. You will need your passport when changing money or travellers' cheques.

Credit cards: All major credit cards are accepted throughout the islands in banks, the larger hotels, travel agents and exchange offices.

Tipping: Tipping is not obligatory in the Canaries as a service charge is generally added to hotel and restaurant bills. Porters, hotel staff, taxi drivers and guides, however, will expect a small gratuity. Known on the islands as a *propina*, a small tip is also expected by waiters in restaurants and it is usual to leave a few coins after having a drink and tapas at a bar.

A service charge is generally added to food bills, but it is customary to leave some small change, between 5–10% of the bill.

Accommodation

Most resorts throughout the islands have a range of hotels from super-luxury with all facilities to pensions which are full-board only. Hotels are categorized from five stars for luxury hotels, through modest hotels (hostales) to pensions or hostels, which are classed as one-star. Aparthotels often have the usual facilities but there are also self-catering rooms which have cooking facilities. Hotels described as *residencias* have no restaurant, but often serve breakfast. The state-run Paradores, located on each island, are generally located in fine mansions, or in places of interest to tourists. Gran Canaria and Tenerife have official camping sites but there is no objection at all to camping anywhere on the islands except in the National Parks.

Eating Out

Most towns and cities have a wide range of restaurants, bistros and cafés, catering to a wide variety of international or local tastes, as do the resort areas. Eating places inland on the islands, or away from villages, are not so common and, away from tourist areas, will concentrate on local cuisine. Lunch generally starts from 14:00 and evening dinner from 20:00. Fish restaurants are common-place and good value for money, as is most food in the Canaries. There are a few designated picnic sites known as *zonas recreativas*.

Transport

Air: Inter-island flights connect airports on every island except La Gomera.

Ferries: Every island is served by regular ferry services mostly run by Compania Transmediterranea.

Buses: There are fast, cheap, regular bus services on Gran Canaria and Tenerife. Those on the other islands are less reliable and hitch-hiking is commonplace. For a 40% discount on cash bus fares, buy a 'bond' ticket from the local tourist office, otherwise buy your ticket on board.

Car Hire: In theory you must have an International Driving Licence if driving in the Canaries or renting a car but in practice valid driver's licences are accepted.

Taxis: Taxis are metered, but there are set-rates for long distances and tours.

Road Rules: In the Canary Islands you drive on the right, overtake on the left and give right of way to traffic coming from the right. Seatbelts must be worn at all times and children under the age of ten must travel in the back of the car. Always carry your driving licence. As the police can demand to see your passport at any time, it is a good idea to carry photocopies of the relevant pages around with you. By law you must carry a set of spare bulbs for your headlamps and rear lights and a regulation warning triangle.

If you take your own car to the islands you will need an International Driving Licence, car registration papers, a nationality sticker, a red warning triangle, a Green

ROAD SIGNS	
alquilar • to hire	
alto • stop	
altopista • highway	
camino cerrado • road closed	
ceda el paso • give way	
camion • lorry	
carro • car	
circamvalacion • bypass	
cruce • crossroads	
cuidado • warning	
curva peligrosa • dangerous bend	
derecha • right	
derecho • straight on	
direccion unica • one-way	
gasolina • petrol	
goma • tyre	
izquierda • left	
no adelantar • no overtaking	
no parquero • no parking	
pare • stop	
parquero • car park	
petroleo • petrol	
ponchera • puncture	
reduzca velocidad • reduce speed	
salida departure • exit	
semaforo • traffic lights	
servicentro • services	

Card extension to your insurance policy and a bail bond. Speed limits are 120kph (75mph) on motorways; 100kph (70mph) on dual carriageways; 90kph (55mph) on other roads, but 60kph (35mph) in built-up areas. Seat belts must be worn on all roads outside built-up areas. Roads vary from multilane motorways to dirt tracks in rural areas, where you are

likely to encounter donkeys and carts. The main cities can be quite congested.

Driving hints: Overheating in hot weather is a common problem so check the water level in the radiator regularly. If your engine has run dry, let it cool down before topping up with water or you will cause severe engine damage. If the radiator is overheating, allow the water in it to cool first before attempting to remove the radiator cap.

Petrol can vaporize in the fuel lines, fuel pump or carburettor, during the prolonged ascents or in high temperatures. Should this happen, let the engine cool down (a damp cloth over the engine will speed up the process).

Take spare water and oil on journeys, check you've the necessary documents and accessories and carry enough money to pay for on the spot fines (for parking offences, traffic violations, etc). Avoid drinking and driving.

Breakdowns and Accidents In the event of a breakdown, it is illegal to tow one car behind another. Minor accidents are not generally reported to the police. A car may be impounded by the police after any serious accident until the legalities have been completed. Whatever the accident, car registration details, names and addresses are best exchanged and, if the car is hired, report any incident to the hire firm and insurance company.

Maps: Good road maps of the Canary Islands are available in most European languages. There are many detailed maps of the larger towns and cities. The best source for maps of the islands are the Spanish Tourist Offices. Bookshops throughout the islands sell maps, including useful street maps. Local tourist information centres will provide you with free guide pamphlets and information leaflets. Also available in this series is the *Globetrotter Travel Map of the Canary Islands* (New Holland).

Business Hours
Most offices, whether they are government or commercial (including the shops), are open from 09:00–13:00 and 15:00–19:00 on weekdays, 09:00–13:00 on Saturdays.

Time Difference
The Canary Islands keep to Greenwich Mean Time in winter and so maintain a one-hour difference with Continental Time. The clocks go back one hour in summer.

Communications
Telephones: The Canary Islands are divided into two for administrative purposes, and so the telephone codes vary from island to island. Gran Canaria, Fuerteventura and Lanzarote have the prefix 928. Tenerife, La Palma, La Gomera and El Hierro are prefixed 922. The area code now should be dialled as part of

the telephone or fax number. Police emergency number is **091** or **092**. Ambulance **061**.
Post: When posting mail to an address in the Canaries write your name and address on the back of the envelope or package together with the word *remitente*.

The postal service is rather slow and laid back. Stamps

USEFUL PHRASES

Desayuno
● *Breakfast*
Comida
(de Mediodia) ● *Lunch*
Cena ● *Dinner*
Cuanto vale?
● *How much is it?*
Si ● *Yes*
Non ● *No*
Buenas dias
● *Good morning*
Buenos tardes
● *Good afternoon*
Buenos noches
● *Good night*
De nada
● *You're welcome*
Adios ● *Goodbye*
Bien venido ● *Welcome*
Por favor ● *Please*
Gracias ● *Thank you*
Bueno ● *Good*
Propina ● *Tip*
Aeropuerto ● *Airport*
Cerrado ● *Closed*
Abierto ● *Open*
Officina de Correos
● *Post Office*
Farmacia ● *Chemist*
Finca ● *Farm*
Calle ● *Street*
Ciudad ● *Town*
Gasolina ● *Petrol*

(*sellos* or *timbres*) can be purchased from Post Offices (*correos*) and from many postcard shops, tobacconists, hotels and some bars. Post boxes are painted yellow. Any urgent mail should be sent either with a reliable traveller or by one of the international courier companies.

Electricity
Most tourist hotels are serviced by a 100 volt system, but 220–240 volts is the norm throughout the islands. A two-pin (round) electric adaptor is recommended for travelling to the islands.

Weights and Measurements
The metric system is in use throughout the islands.

Health Services
Citizens of EU countries are entitled to free medical treatment (except dental), and, for UK visitors, an E111 Form should be obtained before travelling. This should be presented to the office in most cases. In the event of **illness and injury** there are hospitals in all major towns as well as many privately run medical clinics throughout the islands. Chemists or *farmacias* display a green cross outside their shops and at least one per town will stay open all night. Notices of which pharmacists are on duty are posted in the chemists windows and in local newspapers.

GOOD READING

• Cioranescue, Alejandro (1980) *La Canarien, the text of Gadifer de la Salle and Jean de Béthancourt.* Tenerife.
• Dicks, Brian (1988) *Lanzarote, Fire Island.* Dryad, London.
• Glas, George (1764) *History of the Canary Islands.* From the Spanish
• Goulding, John and Margaret (1989) *Lanzarote Windrush.* Lanzarote, Island Guides, Gloucestershire.
• Fernanadez-Armesto (1982) *The Canary Islands after the Conquest.* Clarendon, Oxford.
• Mercer, John (1980) *The Canary Islanders.* Collins, London.
• Stone, Olivia (1887) *Tenerife and its Six Satellites.* Marcus Ward, London.

For the **disabled traveller** there are several tour operators which offer interesting holidays in the Canary Islands. Generally, provision for disabled travellers is poor. Most monuments are not accessible either due to their location, or because of the numerous steps. Public transport is not very well-equipped or prepared for the disabled, nor are most toilet facilities, telephones or any other public facility. The authorities and hotel companies, however, are becoming more aware of the needs of disabled travellers and are gradually adapting their services in order to accommodate them.

Health Precautions

The most common ailments visitors require treatment for are **sunburn** and **dehydration**. Salt pills and quantities of non-alcoholic liquids diminish the effects of too much sun. The sun is at its strongest 11:00–15:00 and you are advised to wear a wide-brimmed hat during the summer. Use a good, expensive sun block. Nausea, lethargy, increased heart beat, headaches and cramps are signs of sunstroke. Take a rehydration solution (sugar, salt and water) and get medical attention. Sunglasses are a must in the hot Canary Islands sun.

Although water is fine for drinking, it is advisable rather to use bottled water outside the tourist resorts. *Agua sin gas* is still water, and *agua con gas* is fizzy water.

Malaria is not a problem on the Islands, but mosquitoes are prevalent and an insect repellant is useful. Cover up well and this is especially applicable in the evenings.

Emergencies

In the case of **emergencies,** it is advisable to call the **police**, tel: **091**.To call the **ambulance** in Gran Canaria Province, tel: (922) 24 59 21. In Tenerife Province, tel: (922) 28 18 00, or **061**.

Fiestas celebrate saints' days and religious occasions, and are usually held between June and September. Each island has several, the traditions and performances of which vary and include rituals which have survived for centuries.

Colourful firework displays, lively horse parades, fiery bonfires, parades of religious icons and traditional folk-dancing and rituals accompany fiestas which often mix pagan customs and religious elements. This is because the islanders have a long-standing dependency on nature, relying on agriculture and the fruits of the sea. Carnivals generally do not have any religious significance, being purely social events for the local community to enjoy. **Ferias** or town fairs are often held in conjunction with the festive and very popular local carnival.

There are many local **public holidays** in the Canary Islands. There are also movable fiestas such as **Maunday Thursday** (Jueves Santo), **Good Friday** (Viernes Santo), **Easter** (Pascua), **Easter Monday** (Lunes de Pascua), and **Corpus Christi**, which can fall in May or July.

INDEX

Birth
without Violence

To you, Yvonne
I wish I could offer
this new translation
but
how could I
since, truly
it is your own child

I wish to express my gratitude to
Yvonne Fitzgerald.
If it had not been for her deep understanding
of babies, her determination, her enthusiasm
and her love of English, this new translation
would never have been written.
And since I feel that all I had been trying
to say about the great mystery which is birth
has at last been fully understood and
expressed in an English that is both literary
and poetical, let me thank her in the name
of all the mothers and, hopefully, all the
doctors and midwives who, once they have
become aware of the ordeal it is to be born,
will meet the young newcomer with more
sensitivity, more intelligence and
more respect.

Frédérick Leboyer

Foreword

From the first time I read this book about fourteen years ago to the present day, it has always been with me.

Over the years I would pick it up again and again and each time discover something new, something I hadn't been able to see or understand earlier, and as I myself progressed through life, so did my understanding of this book deepen. All through these years I always felt that the English version did not do the book justice, especially when I read and began to know the original French edition.

With this in mind, and since the book had sadly disappeared from most bookshops, I proposed to Frédérick Leboyer that we should make a new translation together, he with his deep knowledge of what he wanted to say, and I with my love of English, and all my experience from the story of my own birth and the birth of my two children.

Frédérick Leboyer spoke as someone who had once been the baby in this book. On my side, I too have been the baby in this book, but years later came another knowledge of birth. On the day that I gave birth myself I had the feeling that it was "I" that was being born as well as the baby.

Slowly it dawned on me that to be born and to give birth are one and the same; that the very act of giving birth takes a woman back to the moment of her own birth.

This new perception of time, of finding oneself outside the limits of time as we know it, can be very confusing. One becomes aware that giving birth takes place in an altered state of consciousness.

Birth, death, dying, being born or giving birth nearly all merge at times, all become the same adventure into and out of that territory we might call no-man's-land.

Because this book throws light onto all these mysteries it remains for me a classic.

Like any mystical text, or in the practice of martial arts, the further you go yourself, the more layers and levels you uncover and the more you come to know yourself, the more this book will come and meet you, the more it will give you.

Yvonne Fitzgerald

Birth
without Violence

Part One

To be born is to Suffer.

— GAUTAMA

1

"Do you think babies like being born?"

"What do you mean, like to be born?"

"Exactly what I said. Do you think children are
happy to come into this world?"

"Happy? But a newborn baby doesn't feel anything.
So it's neither happy nor unhappy."

"How do you know that?"

"Well, it's obvious. Everyone knows that."

"That's not much of a reason, is it?"

"I suppose you're right. But all the same, they
don't really see or hear properly, do they?"

"And that makes you think they don't feel anything
either?"

"Of course, they don't."

"Then why do they cry so bitterly?"

"Well, that's to expand their lungs, isn't it?"

"Expand their lungs! That hardly explains it.
My goodness, don't tell me you've never heard a
newborn baby cry!"

"Yes, of course I have. But that doesn't necessarily mean
he's suffering."

"Do you think he's expressing his pleasure, his delight at
being with us?"

"I don't think it's either of those things. I
told you, babies don't feel anything."

"And what makes you so sure? If I may ask once more."
"Well, for a start, they're so small. I mean, at
that age . . ."
"How can an intelligent person like you say that!
As if size had anything to do with it. Small!
As for age, have you forgotten that, the younger you
are, the more intensely you feel? Young children
suffer agonies about things that seem quite trivial
to us because they feel a thousand times more than
we do. This is the blessing and at the same time
the curse of their heightened sensitivity."
"Well, you could be right. But, all the same, it's
still hard to understand that they can feel, I mean
there is no real consciousness at that stage, is
there?"
"Consciousness? You mean they have no soul?"
"No, no. I don't mean a soul. I don't know anything
about the soul."
"But, consciousness? You know about consciousness?
Wonderful! At last I have found someone who can
explain this great mystery to me. My friend, I am
on my knees. Tell me, please tell me. What is
consciousness?"
"Well . . . actually . . . well, you see,
well . . . consciousness . . ."

2

Let's not continue this discussion.
Arguing is refusing to see things as they are.
Things, that is to say, facts.
The simple fact is that as soon as a child is
born he starts to cry and how bitterly.
And although this is very strange, it is the one
thing that delights everyone there.
"How beautifully my child cries!"
exclaims the happy mother, thrilled and amazed that
something so little can make so much noise.
Does this crying simply mean that all the reflexes
are normal and that the machine works?
So man is nothing but a machine?
Or could the cries be trying to express some pain,
some terrible sorrow.
If the baby is crying with such intensity doesn't it
mean that he's suffering terribly?
Could childbirth be as distressing for the child as
for the mother?
And if so, does anyone care?
It doesn't seem so, judging by the way we treat
the new arrival.

Alas, it seems a deeply rooted idea that "it"
doesn't see anything, "it" doesn't hear anything.
How, then, could "it" feel anything like sorrow
or pain?
The answer is simple:
"it" cries, "it" screams,
in short,
"it"
is an object.

And what if, by any chance,
"it"
is already
a person?

3

The newborn baby . . . a person?
Now, really.
Medical books will tell you quite the opposite.
Books . . .
How often does the scientific truth of one day become
the lie of the next.
So how do we know what is what?
Looking at the facts,
that is to say, asking the person concerned, the
child, might give us the answer.
The trouble is that a newborn baby can't speak.
And yet when you think of all the noise they make,
it's hard to say they cannot express themselves.
If a Chinese man breaks his leg, although you may not
speak a word of Chinese, you can understand his
screaming perfectly.
And when it comes to screaming, who in the world
can scream like a newborn baby?

And if you won't take my word for it,
see for yourself.

4

What else is there to say?
The tragic forehead, the screaming mouth, these
closed eyes, clenched eyebrows, these desperate,
pleading, outstretched hands, these feet,
furiously kicking, the legs curled up to protect
the tender stomach, this flesh which is nothing but
a mass of spasms, jolts . . .
How could you say that a baby doesn't speak when
with his whole being he's protesting:
"Don't touch me! Don't touch me! Leave me
alone!"
And at the same time begging:
"Help me! Somebody please help me!"

Has there ever been such despair in one voice?
This child is in agony.
But nobody even hears it.
Isn't that extraordinary?

5

"Do you mean to say that . . . the reason this baby is
crying so bitterly . . . do you think he's trying to
tell us . . ."
"Your mind will use any trick in order to block out
what it really means to be born.
Looking at the pictures we've seen, people might say:
'But that's not a normal birth. This baby is being
tortured by sadists!'
Sadists?
No.
Just ordinary people like you and me.
And if you don't believe me,
just look. Just see."

6

The Holy Family.
In its modern version, that is.
A child has just been born. The mother and father
look on delightedly. Even the young obstetrician
smiles. The same look of wonder and happiness
lights up all their faces.
Everyone is radiant with happiness.
Everyone except the child.
The child?
You hadn't even noticed the child, had you?

Oh no! This can't be true!
This mask of indescribable agony, these hands
clutching, clinging onto this head, like someone
struck by lightning, shattered, who at any moment
is going to fall to the ground, like a mortally
wounded soldier.

This . . . a birth?
It's a murder.

And in the midst of all this suffering,
the parents . . . in rapture!

But it can't be true!
No! It can't be true!
And yet, it is true.
Yes, this is birth

for the child.

7

Isn't it amazing how blind we can be?
Let us try to understand why.
Actually it is simple.
Take the young doctor; what is he smiling about?
The happy child?
Not exactly.
"His" delivery has been a success. Mother and baby
are doing well, so this man is pleased.
Pleased with himself, that is to say.
And the mother?
Blissfully happy as she smiles at her baby.
Maybe she's smiling because it's over.
She's done it!
She's very relieved, and more than anything, she's
proud.
Proud of herself most probably.
The father?
This man who has more than likely never done very much
out of the ordinary, has managed to produce (or so he
is thinking!) a son and heir!
A small heir who's going to carry on the accomplishments
of his parents!
Of course he's proud!

In fact, you could say everyone is delighted.
All delighted with themselves,
except . . .
the child.

8

Isn't it a tragedy?

We should be crying tears of shame, crying for our own blindness.

The same blindness that made us think women had to suffer simply because we didn't know any better.

Happily we no longer believe in the old saying:

"In pain shall ye give birth."

Isn't it time to do for the child what we've been trying to do for the mother?

9

But what can be done for this poor child?
Are we to look to the amazing advances in modern
technology for the answer?
No. Quite the contrary.
It was only when we asked what caused a woman to suffer
when she gives birth that we began to see it was
her FEAR that made her fight and tighten up, lock
herself into the vicious circle:
the more pain, the more fear,
the more fear, the more pain.
With the same simple approach let's try and
understand what makes the child suffer.

Part Two

1

To be born is to suffer.
Birth is pain.
For the woman, as we all know, and for the child
as we have forgotten.
Now that we are finally aware of it, let us try to
understand why.
What is it that makes being born such a horror?

2

The nightmare of being born is not so
much the pain as the fear.
For the baby, the world is a terrifying place.
It is the vastness, the enormity of the whole
experience of being born which so terrifies this little traveler.
Blindly, madly, we assume that the newborn baby feels
nothing.
In fact, he feels . . . everything.
Everything, totally, completely, utterly,
and with a sensitivity we can't even begin to
imagine.
Birth is a tempest, a tidal wave of sensations
and he doesn't know what to make of them.
Sensations are felt more acutely, more strongly by the child,
because they are all new, and because his skin is
so fresh, so tender,
while our blunted deadened senses have
become indifferent.
The result of age, or maybe of habit.

3

Let's begin with sight.
A newborn baby cannot see.
Or so we are told in books, and have come to believe.
Otherwise, we could never
shine a light straight into the eyes of a newborn baby
as we do.
What if we were to lower the lights as the child is being
born?
But why lower lights for someone who
is blind?

Blind?
Maybe it is time that
we
opened our eyes.

If we did, what might we see?
Just as the head emerges, while the body is still
prisoner, the child opens his eyes wide. Only to
close them again instantly, screaming, a look of
indescribable suffering on his tiny
face.

Are we trying to brand our children with the marks of
suffering, of violence
by blinding them as we do with dazzling lights?
What goes on before a bullfight?
How is a furious charging bull produced, mad with
pain and rage?

He is locked up in the pitch dark for a week
then chased out into the blinding light of the arena.
Of course he charges! He's got to kill!
Perhaps there lurks a murderer in the heart of
every man as well. Is it surprising?

4

Now hearing.
Do you imagine a newborn child is deaf?
No more than he's blind.
By the time he arrives in this world he's been
aware of sound for a long time. He already
knows many sounds from the universe which is his mother's
body:
intestines rumbling, joints cracking,
and that spellbinding rhythm, the heartbeat,
even nobler, grander,
the throbbing undercurrent, the swell,
sometimes the storm
that is "her" breath.
Then . . . "her" voice, unique in
its quality, its mood, its accent, its inflections.
Out of all of which is woven, as it were, this child.
From a great distance come the sounds of the
outside world.
What a symphony!

But remember that all these sounds are muffled,
filtered, cushioned by the waters.
So that once the child is out of the water, how the
world roars!
Voices, cries, any small sounds in the room
are like a thousand thunderclaps to the unhappy
child!
It is only because we are unaware, or because we have
forgotten how acute the sensitivity of a newborn baby is
that we dare talk at the top of our voices or even, at times,
shout out orders in a delivery room.

Where we should be as spontaneously and respectfully
silent as we are in a forest or a church.

5

Now we begin to suspect what a calamity,
what a disaster it can be to be born,
to arrive suddenly into the midst of all this
ignorance, all this unintentional cruelty.
What about the newborn baby's skin?
This timorous skin that quivers at the slightest
touch, this skin that knows if what approaches is
friend or foe and can start to tremble,

this skin, raw as an open wound, which until this moment
has known nothing but the caress of the friendly
waves lapping it.
What is in store for it now?
Roughness, insensitivity
the macabre deadness of surgical gloves,
the coldness of aluminum surfaces,
the towels, stiff with starch.
So the newborn baby screams,
and we
laugh delightedly.

6

Once the scales begin to fall from our eyes
and we become aware
of the torture we've made of birth,
something in us cannot but shout
"Stop! Just stop!"

Hell is no abstraction.
It exists.
Not as a possibility in some other world at
the end of our days,
but here and now, right at the start.
Who would be surprised to learn that such visions
of horror haunt us for the rest of our days?

Is that it then?
Is that the extent of the torture?
No.

There is fire, which burns the skin, scalds the eyes,
engulfs the whole being, as if this poor baby had
to swallow this fire.
Think back to your first cigarette, or your
first whiskey, and remember the tears it brought
to your eyes, how your choking breath protested.
Such a memory might begin to help you understand how
the baby feels drawing in his first gulp of air.
Of course the baby screams, his whole being
struggling to expel this vicious fire,
to fight bitterly this precious air, which is
the very substance of life!

So it all begins with a "NO!"
to life itself.

7

If even that were the end of the suffering,
the pain.
But it isn't.

No sooner is the child born, than we grasp his feet
and dangle him upside down in mid-air!
To get a sense of the unbearable
vertigo the child experiences, we must go
back a bit, back to the womb.

8

In the womb the child's life unfolded like
a play in two acts;
two seasons, as different as summer from
winter.
In the beginning, the "golden age."
The embryo, a tiny plant, budding, growing
and one day becoming a fetus.
From vegetable to animal; movement appears,
spreading from the little trunk outward, to the extremities.
The little plant has learned to move its branches,
the fetus is now enjoying his limbs.
Heavenly freedom!
Yes, this is the golden age!
This little being is weightless; free of all shackles,
all worries.

Carried weightless by the waters,
he plays,

he frolics,
he gambols,
light as a bird,
flashing as quickly, as brilliantly as a fish.

In his limitless kingdom,
in his boundless freedom,
as if, passing through the immensity of time,
he tries on all the robes,
he tastes and enjoys all the forms
which Life has dreamed up for Itself.

Alas, why must it be that everything must become
its own opposite?
This is, unfortunately,
the Law,
to which all things must bow.
So it is that, dancing in tune to this Universal
Breath,
Night leads towards Day,
Spring to Winter.
It is the inevitable law that turns the enchanted
garden where the child once played so freely
into a garden of shadows and sorrow.

During the first half of pregnancy the egg
(that is to say the membranes which surround and contain
the fetus, and the waters in which he swims) has
been growing more quickly than the child.
But from now on the reverse becomes true:
the fetus is now growing much bigger, becoming
a little child.
The egg does the opposite. It has achieved its own
perfection and hardly grows any more.

Because he is growing so large, one day the child
comes upon something solid: the walls of the uterus,
and learns for the first time that his kingdom has
boundaries.
Because he keeps on growing, the space around him
becomes more and more confined.
His world seems to be closing in on him,
gripping him in its clutches.
The former absolute monarch must now reckon with the
law!
Careless freedom, golden hours!
My foolish youth!
Where have you gone?
Why have you left me?

The child, once his own master, now becomes a
prisoner.
Immured.
And what a prison.
Not only do the walls press in on him,
squashing him from all sides,
but the floor is coming up to meet him,
even as the ceiling is descending slowly,
relentlessly, forcing his neck to bend.
What is there for him to do but bow his head in submission,
accept this abasement.
And wait.

9

But one day he is rewarded for his
humility.
To his surprise the grip is now an embrace.
The walls are suddenly alive, and the clutch has become
a caress!
What's happening?
His fear is changing into pleasure!
Now he revels in the very sensations that first made
him tremble.
When they come he quivers with pleasure,
curves his back,

bends his head
and waits,
but this time, with anticipation, with wonder.

What is happening? . . .
What is the reason for all this?
Contractions.
The contractions of the final month of pregnancy,
warming the uterus, preparing it for its new role.

But then one day . . .
the gentle waves lash into a storm . . .
and there is anger in this embrace!
It's grinding, crushing, instead of holding,
cherishing!
The once pleasant game has become horrible. . . .
It's not being caressed, it's being hunted.
I thought you loved me,
but now you're squeezing me, killing me,
pushing me down.
You want me to die,
to launch myself into . . . this emptiness,
this bottomless pit!

With all the strength he can muster,
the child resists.

Not to leave, not to go, not to jump . . .
anything . . . but not this void.
He's fighting not to be cast out, not to be expelled,
and of course he's going to lose.

His back stiffens, his head hunches down
into his shoulders,
his heart thumps as if it will break, the child
is nothing but a mass of terror.
The walls are closing in on him like a
wine press crushing grapes.
His prison has become
a passageway,
which is turning into a funnel.

As for his terror, which is limitless,
it has turned into rage.
Animated by rage,
he's going to attack.
These walls are trying to kill me,
they must give way!
And these walls are . . .
my mother!
My mother who carried me,
who loved me!

Has she gone mad?
Or have I?
This monster won't let go.
My head, oh my poor head,
this poor head which bears the brunt
of all this misery.
It's going to explode.

The end is in sight.
It must mean death.
How can he know, this poor, unhappy child,
that the darker the gloom, the obscurity,
the closer he is to reaching
the light, the very light of life!

10

It is then that everything seems to
become chaos!
The walls have released me, the prison, the dungeon
has vanished.
Nothing!
Has the entire universe exploded?
No.
I am born . . .
and around me,
the void.

Freedom, unbearable freedom.
Before, everything was crushing me, killing me, but at
least I had shape, I had some form!
Prison, I cursed you!
Mother, oh my mother, where are you?
Without you, where am I?
If you are gone
I no longer exist.
Come back, come back to me,
Hold me! Crush me!
So that I may be!

11

Fear always strikes from behind.
The enemy always attacks you from the rear.
The child is wild with anxiety
for the simple reason that he is not being held
any more.
His back, which has been curled up for months,
which the contractions have drawn taut as a bow,
is suddenly released,
like a bow having let fly its arrow.
But what a shock!
To calm, reassure and pacify the
terrified child, we must gather up his little body,
hold it back from the void, save it from this unwanted

liberty, which he cannot yet taste or enjoy,
because it came all at once, and far too quickly.
We must help him the same way we regulate the air pressure
for a deep sea diver who has surfaced too fast.

What fools we are!
Instead of gathering up the little body,
we hang it by its feet, leaving it swinging in the void.
As for the head, this poor head,
which has borne the brunt of the catastrophe,
we let it dangle, and give the poor child the sense
that everything is whirling, spinning,
that the universe holds nothing but unbearable vertigo.

12

Next, where do we put this martyr, this child
who comes from the security, the warmth of the womb?
we put him onto
the freezing harshness of the scales!
Steel, hard and cold, cold as ice,
cold which burns like fire.
A sadist couldn't do better.
The baby screams louder and louder.
Yet everyone else is in rapture.
"Listen! Listen to him cry!" they say,
delighted at all the noise he's making.

Then he's off again.
Carried by his heels of course.
Another trip, more vertigo.
He's put somewhere on a table and we abandon him, but not
for long.
Now for the drops.
It wasn't enough to stab his eyes with light
directed right onto his face, now we've got something
even worse in store for him.
Since we are the adults, we are the stronger,
we decide . . .

13

Of course, we prevail.
We force the tender eyelids open,
to apply a few drops of burning liquid. . . .
Drops.
Drops of fire, supposed to protect him from an
infection long since eradicated.
As if he knows what's coming,
he struggles like one possessed,
he squeezes his eyelids tightly together
trying desperately to protect himself.

14

Then he's left on his own.
Adrift in this incomprehensible, insane, hostile
world,
which seems bent on destroying him.
Escape! Escape!
Suddenly an amazing thing happens:
at the limit of his tears, the limit of his breath,
at the limit of his misery, the newborn finds a way
to escape.
Not that his legs can take him anywhere, but
he can flee to within himself.
Arms and legs clasped, curled up into a ball,
almost as though he were a fetus again.
He has rejected his birth, and the world as well.
He's back in paradise,
willing prisoner in a symbolic womb.

15

But his precious moments of peace don't last
long.
He must be elegant, reflect well on his mother!
So for her sake he is squeezed into those implements of
torture we call clothes.

16

The glass has been drained to its dregs.
The worn-out, defeated child gives up.
He lets himself fall back into the arms of his only
friend,
his one refuge:
sleep.

17

This torture, this slaughter of an innocent,
this murder
is what we have made of birth.
But how naive, how innocent to imagine
no trace will remain;
that one could emerge unscathed, unmarked, from
such an experience.
The scars are everywhere:
in our flesh, our bones, our backs,
our nightmares, our madness,
and all the insanity, the folly of this world—
its tortures, its wars, its prisons.

Of what else do all our myths and legends cry,
all our holy scriptures,
if not of this tragic odyssey.

Part Three

The answer is in the question.

1

We were wondering about how best to prepare the
child . . .
Now we can see it's not the child who needs
to be prepared.
It is ourselves.
It is our eyes that need to open,
our blindness that has to stop.
If we used just a little intelligence,
how simple things could be.

2

In short, everything begins in paradox.
The child was in prison,
and as soon as he's free,
he yells!
This, they say, often happens to prisoners.
We open the cell doors,
and the freedom makes the prisoners disoriented,
goes to their heads!
In fact, they begin to behave as if they missed
their cells, their jail, and would prefer to be locked up
again!
And unconsciously they do everything they
can to find themselves once more safely behind bars!
In the same way, seeing the newborn baby panic-stricken

by his freedom, you feel like saying:
"Why are you crying?
You are absolutely miserable when you should be
rejoicing!
Try and understand what's happened,
so you can enjoy your new freedom!
See how you can stretch yourself,
play and move around!
What are you crying about?"

At that point everything seems to be in a state of
complete confusion, almost impossible to repair.
And yet it is all very simple.
As we shall see.

To communicate we must speak to the child in a language
he can understand, one which doesn't rely on words
and yet may be understood by anyone.
Love.
Speak . . . the language of love . . . to a newborn!
Why, yes, of course!
How else do lovers communicate?
They don't say anything, they simply touch.
Because they are modest and shy, they shun the
light,

prefer darkness, night.
In obscurity, in silence, they
reach for each other, wrapping their arms around
each other, they re-create the old prison,
in which they feel safe, protected
from the world outside.
Their hands speak,
and it is their bodies that understand.

So this is the way to talk to the newborn:
in silence and darkness,
with gentle but loving hands,
that reassure and move slowly,
and in time with his breathing.

But let us go step by step,
sense by sense as it were.

3

Let us begin with sight.
Like lovers, let's turn down the lights.
Who could make love under a spotlight?
Therefore let's keep only the least light—a candle
for instance—for the sake of the doctor's vision.
How peaceful, how calming this half light is,

and so much in keeping with the mother's own inner silence.

4

Now hearing.
Nothing could be simpler; all we have to do is remain silent.
Simple?
Perhaps it's not as easy as it sounds at first.
The mind is so noisy.
It is not always easy to stay silent in the company of others.
One has a tendency to think of something and feel impelled to say it.
Yet it is only if we pay attention to the other, and to our own depths, that we will experience that something beyond words.
But silence is not something that comes spontaneously to us, rather we must search for this and call it up from deep within us.
In fact, the first women who experienced silence in childbirth found it so new that they were disturbed, even frightened.

As the end of labor is approaching, there should be

very few words spoken in the room.
In the quiet you can feel that you are coming
very close to something of gravity.
The silence will be like the hush that settles over the room
of someone who is dying.
Perhaps it is the same threshold we cross,
whether coming or going.

Such an almost tangible silence has a most powerful
effect on the child, although how or why cannot
be explained.
Yet it dispels the panic,
holds back the fear that was waiting to
surge up within the child.
Of course, at times it is necessary to say something,
to give an instruction.
This must be whispered, almost
inaudible.
When we first attempted this,
our hushed voices took women so completely by
surprise, that they were overtaken
by panic. In this intense
silence all the mothers could hear . . . was that
they couldn't hear anything!
The children responded spontaneously to
this tranquility.

But the mothers' eyes, as they darted from one
face to another, begging for an answer,
told of the women's surprise.
Unable to hold back, they burst out:
"Why isn't my baby crying?"
It was agonizing.
It was astounding. It was heartbreaking.
"Why isn't my baby crying?"
It was like the cry of an inconsolable child whose toy was
not what he had been hoping for.

We had not thought it necessary to tell the
mothers beforehand that their babies probably would
not cry.
And because this silence seemed so pleasing to us,
it had never occurred to us that it might frighten
the mothers.
But
"My child isn't alive!" would wail the despairing
voice.
It was ludicrous.
"Your child is fine!" we would whisper.
The whispering made things worse.
"What are you whispering about? Is my baby dead?

Oh, no! My baby is dead!"
Dead! Even as the child was wriggling and moving
on her belly.
"Stop!" we would say. "Dead people don't move!
Can't you feel your child moving; can't you sense
how happy he is?"
But our words went unheard.

All this made us realize that we should have
explained to the mother what was going to
happen. A silent happy newborn is so
new and unexpected, it goes completely
against accepted ideas.

So we tried, although a bit late, to explain
the silence: that it was maintained out of
respect for the child, out of concern for his ears,
that we were quiet because we didn't want to frighten
him with our loud voices. We tried to explain to the
mothers that it is no more necessary for her child to
be born suffering and screaming, than it is that
she go through hell in order to give birth.
Our explanations came too late. Their eyes remained
full of doubt, of regret!

5

This education, this initiation into silence is
just as necessary for all those who
attend the woman when she's giving birth: the
obstetrician, the midwife, the nurses.
People tend to speak loudly in delivery rooms,
often shouting their words of encouragement:
"Come on, push! Push!"
Which is a complete mistake.
Intended as encouragement, these loud exhortations
are instead most disturbing
for the mother.
For a woman in labor is in
what might be called an altered state of
consciousness, and hypersensitive to
the slightest noise or movement around her.

6

Darkness, or almost, and . . . silence.
A profound peace settles in the room.
You can feel the respect which naturally
attends the arrival of a baby.
One doesn't shout in a church.
One spontaneously lowers one's voice.

If there is such a thing as a sanctified place, surely
it is the room the child is about to enter.

Subdued light, silence . . . what else is needed?
Patience.
Or rather, the sense that one should slow down
and thereby enter into another rhythm; the profound
rhythm of life,
to which the mother has spontaneously become attuned,
and which is also the tempo of the child.

Unless you have re-created this incredible languor
in your own body, it is impossible to understand
birth. Impossible to meet the newborn on his terms.
In order to reach this deep understanding, to arrive at
a place where you can meet the child, you have to, as it
were, step out of time.
Step out of *our* time.
Meaning our strong, familiar sense
of how time is flowing, of the apparent speed, with which
for us, it seems to flow.
Our sense of time, and the time sense of the
newborn baby are practically irreconcilable.
The one is a state of near statis,
the other state, ours, is often a frenzied restlessness,
close to madness.
Besides, we adults are never "here."
We are always somewhere else.

In the past, in our memories.
In the future, in our plans.
We're always looking back, at what is gone,
or ahead, at what is yet to happen.
Never focusing on "here and now!"
Yet if we have any hope of rediscovering the newborn
baby,
we must step outside of our own furiously running time.
Which seems impossible.
How can we step out of time?
How can we escape its fast and furious flow?
The only way is by trying to be fully with the present
moment.
Yes, to be here *and* now, as if there were no yesterday, no
tomorrow.
To allow any thought that the moment
will end, that another appointment awaits,
is enough to break the spell.
As usual, everything is very simple.
And apparently impossible.
How can we reconcile the irreconcilable?
How can finite combine with infinite?
It can only happen if we open completely to the other,
which means completely forgetting oneself.

7

Now the stage is set.
The lights are dimmed.
The curtain may rise.
The child can make his entrance.
At last he is here.

8

Head first, and then his shoulders, one after the
other.
Either all this happens naturally, or some help is
needed at this critical moment.
As soon as the head is out the child wants to draw breath,
which is impossible for him because his chest is still
imprisoned in his mother's body.
If the shoulders are stuck, his progress
comes to a halt, and help is needed quickly,
because anguish is building up furiously in
the child.
How can we help?
By sliding a finger under the child's armpit we can help
the rotation of his body and liberate the little prisoner.
Then, holding him under both arms we hoist him
out, as if pulling him from a well, and put him
straight onto his mother's belly.
Most important of all, we never, never, at any time
touch his head.

He's lying on his mother's belly.
And where better to receive the child, this
belly. It is the exact shape to receive
the baby. When he was within, it was rounded and convex,
it has now become hollow, and waits like a nest to cradle
the child.
Soft and supple, it moves with
the rhythm of the mother's breathing,
and the living warmth of her body makes it
the perfect place for the newborn to be.
Finally, and this is most important, because the
baby remains so near to her, the umbilical cord can remain
intact.

9

Cutting the cord the moment a baby has emerged from his
mother's womb is an act of extreme cruelty, and harms
the baby to an extent that is hard to believe.
Leaving it intact, however, so long as it
continues to beat, transforms the whole birth experience.
For one thing, it forces the obstetrician to be
patient, and leads him, as well as the mother, to respect
the rhythm, the sense of time ordained by the child.
Besides, leaving the cord intact allows the
natural physiological changes to take place within the
child's body at their own pace.

We have already described the way air suddenly rushing
into the baby's lungs has the same effect on him
as a burn. But there is more.
Before his birth, the child lived in oneness.
For him there was no difference between
the world and himself, because inside and outside were
one. He knew nothing of polarities. He didn't
know about being cold, for example, because cold
cannot exist without heat. The body temperature of
the mother and the baby are exactly the same. How
then could he appreciate any contrast?

So you might say that before birth, there was neither
inside nor outside, any more than there was hot or
cold.
As he enters this world, the newborn baby encounters
for the first time a kingdom of opposites in which
everything is either good or bad, pleasant or
unpleasant, agreeable or disagreeable, wet or dry.
What is the gate through which he enters this kingdom
of opposites?
Not through his senses, that comes much later,
but through breathing.
When he takes his first breath, he crosses a threshold,
a border.

He breathes in, and from this action is born its
opposite: he breathes out.
And then in turn . . .

Thus he is launched irrevocably into the eternal
cycle, the never-ending oscillation, the very principle
of our world, in which everything comes back to this
breath, this pulsation.
He is in the world where everything, for always,
is born of its own opposite:
day from night, summer from winter,
riches from poverty, strength from weakness,
never ending,
without beginning.

10

To breathe is to become one with the world outside,
to tune to the music of the spheres.
Its function is to make the blood take in oxygen,
and get rid of wastes, mostly carbon dioxide.
But in this simple exchange, two worlds come
near each other, try to mix and touch: the world
of outside and the world of inside.
Two worlds, separated, try to reunite:
the interior world of the organism, the little "I,"
and the exterior world, the vast universe.

It is in the lungs where they meet—the blood
mounting from one's own depths, the air
coming from above.
The blood and air rush to conjoin, anxious
to mix and mingle.
Of course they can't, separated as they are by
the barrier of the alveol membrane.
Both sigh for this lost oneness.

The blood arrives in the lungs, depleted of its
oxygen, its strength spent, dark with waste: the carbon
dioxide which makes it old.
Here it is going to rid itself of its old age, gain its
energy, rejuvenate.
Transformed by this visit to the fountain of youth, it
departs, alive, red and rich!
It returns to the depths where it gives forth its riches.
Once more lets itself be filled with
wastes, and then returns to the lungs. Thus the cycle
continues indefinitely.
As for the heart, it keeps pumping, pushing the blood,
sending it, rich and red towards the thirsty tissues of
the organism, and sending it back when it has
become old and worn-out, for renewal to
the lungs.

How does all this happen in the fetus,
where the lungs are not yet working? The blood of
the fetus, just like ours, needs to be renewed.
The placenta fulfills this role.
Among other things it does, it takes the place
of the lungs.
The blood comes and goes through the umbilical cord,
which contains three conduits, a vein and two arteries,
covered by a sheath.
So, the blood of the fetus renews itself, not
by contact with air, but in the placenta by contact with
the blood of the mother, which in her lungs . . . and so on.

The mother, in effect, breathes for the baby, just as
she eats for him, carries him, protects him, sleeps and
dreams . . .
Yes. The child is completely dependent
before his birth.
But then what happens?
A total upheaval: The blood, that until then flowed
through the cord, suddenly rushes into the lungs!
The child abandons the old route, he leaves the way of
the mother.
In the act of drawing breath, of oxygenating his own blood
with his own lungs, the child becomes himself, in effect
saying, "Woman, what do we have in common?
I no longer need an intermediary between myself and the
world."

Of course it is only a first step, for all the rest he
still relies totally on his mother.
But it's a step in the right direction.
With his first breath, the child sets forth on the road to
independence, to autonomy, to freedom.
But practically speaking much depends on the way
this transition takes place.
Whether this transition is made slowly, progressively, or
brutally, in panic and terror, can make the difference
between a gentle birth
. . . or a tragedy.

11

If the changeover comes abruptly it will leave a mark
for the rest of life. Any future change will always be
perceived as threatening.
Of course, the child must not, at all costs, be deprived
of oxygen, not even for one moment.
Here there is no quarrel with medical science
which agrees perfectly with nature's plan.
Nature provides oxygen for the
child through two sources:
the cord continues to beat, even as the lungs begin to
function.
The two systems work together, one taking over from the
other, like a relay. The first, the cord, continues
to oxygenate the child until the new system, the lungs,
have taken over completely.

Although the child is out of the womb, he remains dependent on his mother through the umbilical cord, which continues to beat strongly for several minutes, four or five, sometimes even longer.

Oxygenated through the cord, and thus protected from anoxia, the child can, without shock or danger, settle down to breathing without being rushed, in his own time.

12

What should we do during these critical few minutes of the transition of the blood from the old route through the placenta to the newly working lungs?

We must understand that Nature herself doesn't take sudden leaps and has her own pace. She has left this time, these few minutes, so that this change over from one world to another can be made with ease.

She has made it so that the baby is oxygenated from two sources for several minutes as, at the same time, an orifice in the heart closes, and the baby is then safely on his own.

For a few minutes the baby straddles two worlds, as it were. Then slowly, slowly he can cross the threshold from one to the other peacefully and easily, and with all safety,

as long as we don't rush in, interfere,
and can manage to quell our old reflexes, our nervousness,
born, in fact, out of the anxiety of our own birth.
The effect on the well-being of the child will be
immeasurable.

We are all so quick to blame Nature, when actually
she's so full of love and wisdom, and it is only we
who are too blind to see.

Whether the cord is cut abruptly or allowed to stop
beating of its own accord completely changes,
even determines the way in which a child perceives his entry
into the world, and, consequently, the way he will react
to the continuous change which is life. You might say
that his perception of this moment will color the rest
of his life.

If we cut the cord immediately, we create a situation
which is the opposite of the one nature intended.
By clamping the cord before the lungs are fully operative
we deprive the child's brain of oxygen.
The organism cannot but react violently to our aggression,
and then a whole system of stress comes into play.
Not only will we have done something absurd and

uncalled for, but we will have set up what Pavlov called a
conditioned reflex which will recur
throughout life.
What have we linked together?
Life and breath,
breath and the fear of impending death.

What geniuses we are!

13

You might then ask how is it that even when the
transition has been allowed to take place in its own
time the child may still give a cry or two?
The answer is simple.
The thoracic cage, now that nothing is compressing it,
suddenly expands, thus creating a void.
The air rushes in and it burns.
Naturally the child tries furiously to expel the air.
This is the first cry.
Then, often, everything stops.
The child pauses, as if dumbfounded by his own suffering.
It can happen that he might repeat the cry two or three
times before this pause.
Then when this pause comes, it is we who
panic. And usually . . . a slap on the bottom

follows. But now that we know better and can control
our impulses, our fears, and trusting the strong beat of
the cord, we can keep our hands to ourselves.
Soon we will see . . .
breathing beginning again of its own accord.
Hesitant at first, timid, careful, it will still pause from
time to time, marking little breaks.
The child, oxygenated as he is by the cord, is pacing himself
and taking in only as much of the burning element
as he can put up with, then pausing, only to start again.
As he gets used to it, he begins to breathe more deeply.

14

Soon he learns to enjoy what, in the beginning, was so
very painful. Very soon, his breathing, which was
at first so hesitant and doubtful, becomes joyous.
In all, the child has given only one or two cries.
All we hear now is a deeply peaceful breathing,
punctuated by short cries, exclamations of surprise,
or even sighs of pleasure.
Mixed with this breath are the sounds the baby
is making with his lips, his nose, his throat.
A language all its own.
And never, never, those screams of terror,
those wails of despair, those hysterical shrieks.
Maybe a child has to give one or two cries when he's
being born,

but must they be cries of anguish?
Because the child is pleased with this new experience,
tasting it in all its newness, he can easily forget the
world he has left behind.
No regrets, not a backward glance.
Coming into life is like waking from a long and pleasurable
sleep, and not from a nightmare.
When the present is so delightful, why cling to the past?

Now that the cord has stopped beating, we can cut it.
Not a sound, no crying, no cause for alarm, not even a
tremor; it has simply become obsolete, and so can be
removed.
An old bond has been left behind.
We have not wrenched the child from his mother,
they have simply parted, and will go their separate ways.
Why would the young traveler yearn for the past
when his voyage ends so happily and he has found the other
bank, so tranquilly, so surely?

How intelligent, what a blessing such a birth is.
Because we left the cord beating it is as if
his mother had accompanied him across the border, and led
him gently into this formidable and forbidding world.
Just as later, when he learns to walk, she will be there
offering him her hand to hold.

An open hand that the child can grasp and let go of as
he takes his first tentative steps.
What a poor mother it would be who suddenly
withdrew her hand the moment her child began to trust his
own strength.

15

Learn to respect this sacred moment of birth,
as fragile, as fleeting, as elusive as dawn.
The child is there, hesitant, tentative,
unsure which way he's about to go.
He stands between two worlds.

For heaven's sake don't touch him,
don't push him,
unless you want him to fall.
Let him wait until he feels
the time is right.

Have you ever watched a bird take flight?
As he's still walking, he's heavy, awkward,
his wings drag, and then suddenly
he's flying,
graceful, elegant and free.
He was the son of earth,
now he's the child of the skies.

Can you say when he left one kingdom for the other?
It is so subtle, the eye can hardly catch it.
As subtle as stepping in,
or out, of time,
to be born,
or to die.

What of the tide,
which imperceptibly,
irresistibly rises,
only to fall.
At what moment did it turn?
Is your ear sharp enough to hear the ocean breathe?

Yes, this birth,
this wave parted from wave,
born from the sea
without ever leaving her.
Don't ever touch it with your rough hands.
You understand nothing of its mysteries.
But the child,
the drop from this ocean,
knows.

A wave pushes him towards the shore,
another pulls him back,
only to push him higher still.
One more,
and he's out of the flood.
He's parted from water,
and come to the land.
He's frightened, terrified.
Let him be.
Just wait.
This child is awakening
for the very first time.

This is his first dawn.
Allow him its grandeur, its majesty.
Don't even stir until he leaves behind
the night and its kingdom of dreams.

16

The rest, you might say, is detail.
Once breathing is well-established, everything is
accomplished.
All has either succeeded or failed.
But details, as always, are not without importance.
For example, in what way should we put the baby on
his mother's belly?
Should we lie him on his side, on his stomach,
or flat on his back?
Never flat on his back.
That would cause the spinal column, which has been
curved for so long, to straighten all at once.
It would suddenly let loose all the dormant energy
locked in there and the shock would be too much. It
would be like an explosion.
Let the child unfold his back when he feels ready
himself.
Don't forget that each child comes equipped with
his own character, his own temperament, his own pace.

There are some, who are no sooner born, than they lift their
heads proudly, draw themselves up, and stretch out
their arms as if to say:
"I'm here!"
These are the strong ones, who settle into their

new kingdom as if they were kings.
Their spines straighten with the force of a
tightly strung bow releasing its arrow.
But sometimes, the very same children will then
withdraw, pull back, frightened by their own
audacity, their own bravery.
There are others, who start off curled up in a little
ball, and only open up little by little, making
their discoveries cautiously.
Because we cannot anticipate what's to come, the best
thing to do is to put the child flat on his belly,
with his arms and legs tucked under him.
This is a familiar posture, the one that
best allows the abdomen to breathe freely and
the baby to work his way, at his own speed, towards
the final unbending.

Then, because the child is on his front,
we can keep an eye on his back, and see how he is
breathing.
In fact, the bending of the spine, of the back, and
the beginning of breathing are all one.
We can watch how breathing takes over the
whole of the baby's body. Not only the chest but
also the belly, and especially the sides.

Very soon the baby is nothing but breath,
which passes like a wave from the top of his head
to the small of his back.
This wave is like the shadow of the contractions
which, like waves themselves, pushed the baby to
the shore.
At the same time it is like watching a tree
start to grow.
Out comes an arm, usually the right, stretching
like the branch of a tree.
Then the other. Both seem surprised that nothing
stops them any more, that space can be so limitless,
so vast.
It's like watching branches grow out of the power of
the breath. The breath is to the child as the sap is to the
tree.
Now the legs.
One after the other, like roots which will one day
stabilize this tree. But not yet. For
the time being they are still very tentative, for
they have had to fight their way out of the
enchanted cave.
In order to allay their panic, all that is needed
is to offer them some limit: an open hand the baby's
feet can meet, offering gentle resistance but
able to be pushed away.

Otherwise, the baby will feel completely
disoriented.
So, little by little, everything settles down,
or rather, everything comes together harmoniously.
Soon, just as if he is waking from his first sleep,
the baby stretches out with a complete sense of his own
well-being.
Since, while all this has been happening, the
cord has stopped beating, we are now ready for the
next step. But let us go slowly, pausing often.

17

Haven't we come a long, long way?
We are out of the water, we have touched dry land.
We've left behind the ever-moving, changing, treacherous
kingdom of the fishes.
Now it is the earth that carries us.
Earth which is steady, tranquil, sound and true.
Earth we can trust.
For the very first time, nothing moves.
What a surprise.
But since there is a price for everything, we now know
for the first time how it feels to be heavy.
We'll have to crawl.
And yet the skies are there, above our heads.

It is their light, their divine light that gave us
the courage to emerge.
And they will give us the courage to stand and walk.

What a long, long road, this path from mineral
to man.
The path each must tread again when he's
come to taste the joy that is life.

What else are we doing when we pray?
Nothing but returning to the source,
the source of all life,
as if going through the whole adventure again.
Wanting to pay homage to Earth, our mother,
we kneel.
With folded arms and a humble heart
we bow to the ground.
Our forehead touching the dust we say
I obey
for I know that, in your wisdom and love
you know better.
There we remain, folded up, empty,
as empty of that precious breath as the child
not yet born who hasn't yet tasted that pleasure of life.
Having paid our respects, expressed our gratitude

to the one who carries us,
to whom we owe everything,
into whose womb we will return at the end of our days,
we arise.

Like a bow
that has let go its arrow,
how vibrant we feel
when, unfolding, we let the air and its joy
fill us full—
as vibrant as we were the day we tasted
our very first dawn.

This, in truth, is prayer.
Since to pray is to be born anew
to the fullness of life.

But then, can one pray in a hurry?
Can it be rushed?
As with the child who's just arrived,
who's joined us,
can't we grant him
a moment of time?

18

A few words about the hands which will hold the newborn
baby.
These hands are the first thing that the child will encounter.
The language they speak is the primal language, the
language of touch.
This is how mother and child were communicating.
It was through the child's back that he
received her messages.
Now that he's born, naked and disoriented,
the way we touch him is crucial.
Most of the time, the hands
of the doctors, the midwives, and the nurses are not gentle
enough.
Simply because they have not realized what it means to
the child.
Because these hands are so unaware, and move much too
quickly, they terrify the child.
Let them be gentle but firm.

Most of all, let them move very, very slowly.
Everything we do for the newborn baby is too rushed, too
hurried for one who is only just entering time.
At this moment, what the child needs is to be massaged,
just as newborn animals need to be licked by their
mothers—the act without which they
often die.

It is most important that the hands that will massage
the baby's back can rediscover the rhythm he knows,
the rhythm of the contractions, the rhythm that moves
with the outward breath.
What the child wants to feel again is not the wild fury,
the storm of labor, but the embracing waves that told him
of his mother's love.
Our hands should travel along his back,
one following the other,
like wave after wave
breaking onto the seashore.
The rhythm of dancers, of lovers.
Love . . . and the child!
Yet what is it lovers are looking for,
if not to heal the rift,
return to the primal sea,
rediscover its infinite pulse.
A return to paradise,
a pilgrimage back to the source.

19

So much for rhythm, for movement.
But there is something else that can be transmitted through
hands, even hands that are not moving.

The child is still so sensitive that he will know by
the feel of the hands resting on him, whether he is
loved or refused, accepted or simply being carelessly
handled.
Under caring hands, the child opens up and lets go.
Whereas, under stiff mechanical hands, he feels
he's being clutched by claws, and of course
he closes up, withdraws in panic, as if to escape to
within himself for protection.

20

Naturally, it's the mother's hands that should hold
the child.
But often she's still overcome by her own
emotions, her own fears, which she's hardly had
time to leave behind.
Her hands are not yet steady and sure.
If someone else, such as a loving midwife, is
there, calm, and able to transmit her inner peace,
her hands would be better in the beginning, until the
mother has had time to catch her breath.
It's not that we want to take the child away from his
mother, but the intensity of what she's just lived
through can still be affecting her so strongly that it
overwhelms the child.
In these crucial moments, the child needs peace,
quiet and calm.

Often mothers don't know how to touch their babies.
Or maybe they just don't dare.
Some deep inhibition seems to hold them back, stop
them.
Why?
Possibly because the child has just come from a part
of the body we don't want to, don't dare to mention.
Perhaps it's our education that makes us step back, as
if this part of us does not exist, or at the
very least, is not something we talk about.
So the mother finds herself in a troubling,
conflict-filled situation, torn between her natural urge,
and her inhibitions, product of her repressive
education.

21

Now let's come back to the child.
The fullness of his breath tells us that all is well.
The cord has been cut.
It is as if centuries have passed and yet it has only
actually been a matter of a few minutes.
What comes next?
However blissful this time has been for mother and
baby, it must come to an end.
The child cannot stay on his mother's belly all his life.

Just as the child had to depart from the womb, now he
will have to leave his mother's body.
To meet with what?
This first step in life cannot be but terrifying.
How can we ease it and pacify this terror?
In the same way that giving a new toy to a child makes it
easier for him to part with the one he's been playing with,
so we must find a way to make him enjoy his first
moment of separation and thus gladly accept that he's on his
own.
Of course we're not going to put him on
ice-cold weighing scales, and even the softest towel
cannot compare with his mother's body.
What could be the answer?
Water.
This is where he has come from, and what he's known
all his life. It's gentle, it's familiar.
It is this very familiarity that in the end
will completely calm him. It will be like
meeting an old friend when one is far from home.
This feeling of something familiar saves the child
who is lost in an overwhelming world of new sensations.
A bath has been prepared in a small tub, filled with
water at body temperature, or slightly higher since
it's going to cool down quickly.
With the permission of the mother, who must be willing,

we take the child,
and slowly, slowly we ease him into the water, feet
first of course.
A sensitive eye can catch how intense the experience is
for the child.
As soon as he finds himself back in water, he becomes
weightless again.
Water has, as it were, once again taken the load of
his body.
His joy and feeling of relief are hard to describe.
We have nearly accomplished a miracle, we have turned
this first separation, which is always loaded with
anguish, and which shadows us all our life, into a joy.
One can feel any remaining tensions in the baby
melt away, vanish under our hands.

And as these tensions melt away,
and what is left of his fear disappears, and
the child feels so safe, he even dares to open his
eyes.
No words can describe the depths of this first look.
It is as if he is asking one and all the questions of man
in that single moment.
Then it becomes so clear that life does not start now, at

this point, but that the child was aware long before
he came to us, and has merely crossed a threshold.
In disagreement with all classical psychology, anyone
who has witnessed such a birth cannot but
exclaim:
"But this child *is* looking! . . ."
Whether he "sees" in the way we do is another
issue.
Maybe we have to accept that there are many ways of
seeing, of knowing.

22

Completely free from fear, and his first surprise over,
he begins to explore his kingdom.
His head turns to the left, to the right, as if
enjoying its new freedom.
Out comes one hand from under the water, it opens and
reaches towards the sky.
Then the other.
His hands move in such harmony you'd think you were
watching
a ballet.
They meet, clasp, and part,
moving with all the grace of an underwater plant.
As for the legs, a little hesitant at first, soon they too
begin to stretch and play.
And here it is important to say that the feet of the

baby should always be able to find the edge of the bath,
to find a limit, as it were. Otherwise, if they meet
with nothing, the child will experience the same panic as
a swimmer out of his depth.

Because his first experience has been so
rich and so pleasant, this baby will always be an
adventurer.
Life, for him, will always be a challenge, which he
will meet with confidence and courage, and an eagerness
to try and taste everything new that
might cross his path.
Is not the constant newness of life, its continual
change and variety, the thing we find
most difficult?

23

Now that fear has subsided, and been left behind once
and for all, let us try to be free of the past and
its fascination.
Let's try to take the step out of the sea,
to land,
and meet with the earth.

Fourth step.
Fourth station of this calvary which is birth,
where there is neither sin or punishment.
It is truly an odyssey,
and the hero, the newborn,
has accomplished something so difficult.

So little by little we begin to take the child out
of the water.
If he doesn't like this idea, and protests,
because once again he's feeling all his own weight,
we don't force him, but lower him back in again,
only to try to take him out a moment later.
Once again he protests,
goes back to the water,
and comes out again,
and what at first seemed unpleasant,
now becomes a game.
This game we play with him,
lifting him out and lowering him back in the water,
is a way of playing with weight and weightlessness.
Isn't it true that no matter the culture,
children all over the world love to
swing,
which makes them, in turn, heavy as a stone, and light as
a bird?

Eventually we lift him out completely,
dry him gently, and swaddle him in something warm,
letting him experience for the first time this feeling that
nothing is moving.
Another new and extraordinary feeling for him.

Remember that all those months he spent inside his
mother, everything was moving, whether his mother
was walking or simply breathing quietly in her
sleep.

24

But now, for the first time . . .
and how strange . . .
nothing is moving at all!
This is the majesty of Earth.
For all those children who have been rushed into the
world, who haven't been led gently from water to land,
from movement to stillness, with so much love,
intelligence and patience, waking up on their own will
always frighten them.
This immobility will always terrify them.
But for the child whose birth has been such a blessing,
these fears will not exist.
He'll be free forever from nightmares and guilt.

25

How impressive it is to watch this child open
his eyes wide, begin to feel his way around,
explore all that surrounds him.
All with no panic, no tears.
On the contrary, with a seriousness, a gravity
that's hard to believe.
Yes, this child is truly like a wise man, an old soul,
because whatever he does, it is with complete
awareness.

But also it seems as if something is emanating
from this child.
He seems to radiate a peace, a serenity, that he's
brought from somewhere far beyond.
The words of Lao Tzu come to mind:

"One who possesses virtue in abundance, the Holy one,
is like a newborn babe."

But what is this "virtue"?
It has nothing to do with morality, being virtuous.
"Virtus" in Latin means courage, vitality, virility.
What Japan and China call Chi,
and India Shakti.
It is the secret, silent power of a Zen Master,

a true Master of Martial Arts,
or a saint.

For one who is sensitive enough to feel it,
sense it,
it is this "virtue,"
this grace,
this Chi, this Shakti
that silently flows,
shines like a blessing
from the newborn.

———

Part Four

*In the pursuit of learning
one knows more every day.
In the pursuit of the way
one does less every day.
Less and less until
one does nothing at all.
And when one does nothing
there is nothing
that's left undone.*

TAO TE CHING

1

Now our story draws to a close.
Now that the child has tasted the joy of being
on his own and the wonder which is stillness,
let him return to his mother.
Not in a panic, not because he's looking for someone,
anyone to save him, as one might cling to any
branch when drowning, or seek any port in a
storm.
No, it is with eyes wide open, in all awareness
and with inner peace that these two will meet.
Lying once again on his mother's body, his ear
against her heart, the child rediscovers the
familiar steady beat.
All is accomplished. All is perfect.
These two who have battled so fiercely are at
peace, at one again.

Maybe we can leave them alone together.
In fact, we should.
To remain would be an indiscretion.
Lovers should not be disturbed.
They don't want anyone to spoil the joy of
intimacy.
Since these two are true lovers, out of
respect and discretion, let us tiptoe from the
room, leaving them to share their new ecstasy.

As for us, we too have come a long way, and learned
so much on the journey.
We were asking: If birth could be as painful, as cruel
for the child as it used to be for most mothers,
What is it that makes the experience so dreadful
for the child?
Now we know.
Since at last, we have understood the message, understood
what the newborn is desperately trying to tell us with
his heartrending screams.
The message is very clear, and very simple indeed:
"I am in pain! I am suffering!"
But more than anything, "I AM AFRAID!"

2

Now we can see that fear and pain are one.
These children are echoing
what their mothers were, for so long, crying in labor.
Of course they never said it directly.
Who has the simplicity, the humility to say
"I am afraid!"?
Yet their poor bodies were nothing but a mass of
spasms, locked muscles, unbearable tensions, frantic
heavings, which bore silent witness to their panic,
their terror.
What could they have been saying but, "I am afraid, I am

terrified!"
By exorcising this fear, women have been freed from the
agony of childbirth and their experience transformed.

In the same way, by sparing the child this fear, this
panic, we can transform birth into an enchantment.

3

Those who are skeptical or simply refuse to change things,
might well say:
"All right. Quite possibly it's far from
pleasant to be born.
But what difference does it make?
It's all over in a few minutes. And afterwards
who remembers? No one.
So then what does it matter how the child is received,
how he is welcomed?"
No one remembers?
Not only is that not true, but it is the complete opposite of
the truth.
The memory of birth and the terror that accompanies it
remains in each one of us.
But since it is so loaded with fear and pain, it
lies dormant and totally repressed, like a dreadful
secret at the bottom of our unconscious, like a

ship on the ocean floor.
But it is there, although we don't always know it.
Just like a name can be in our memory, but if it is
linked with unpleasant overtones, we think we can't
remember it.
Then again you might say if it is buried so deeply,
why dig it up, why not just let it rest?
Maybe we can't.
It is constantly trying to surface, and expresses itself
in our nightmares, our myths, our most
secret irrational inhibitions.
One could almost say that the root of all anguish
is an unconscious memory of birth and its
terrors.
Only those who have forgotten how it feels to wake up
at night, overwhelmed with panic, and the feeling that
lions and tigers were roaring under their bed,
ready to pounce, would deny the devastating
intensity of such fears, which are in fact nothing but
shadows of the original fear: the fear which is birth.

4

Fear.
How few of us are aware of how
much unconscious fear there is in our lives!

All this fear linked with the horror which is
birth.

One can only imagine what it would be like to be born
without this fear
or with this fear immediately extinguished like a fire
that's caught before it
gets a hold and becomes out of control.
Yes, if this fear could be extinguished before it can take
hold, how extraordinary life would be for one
so blessed.
The point of this book, of this whole story, is not just
to make birth something nice. It is far, far more
ambitious: it amounts to nothing less than a plan to give
birth to heros, those extraordinary beings who seem free of
fear, and so can drink fully from the cup of life.

5

A plaguing question was why it seemed no one
was ever concerned about the child's plight, and even
ignored his anguish and despair.
Maybe there is something there that we ourselves do not
want to look at,
possibly because it might awaken something unpleasant
deep within ourselves that we'd rather not know about:
our own fear of death.

Strange, isn't it, that there seems to be such a deep
secret link between birth and death?
It is as if the fear of death, the dark shadow that casts
its gloom over our whole lives, is nothing but the
unconscious memory of . . . the fear we felt when
we were born.
So that . . . but then it's nearly too good to be true . . .
one born free of this fear would travel
through life as free as a bird.

6

Is this why we cut the cord in such a senseless, untimely
way?
Well, you might say, it's with the idea that it's going
to make the child breathe.
Why are we so anxious that he should breathe?
Of course there is the rational answer: lack of oxygen
will damage the brain—which is quite true.
But, as always, behind rationality is a deeper,
hidden reason.
Although no one is aware of it, those attending, watching
a baby being born, unconsciously, unknowingly
"hold their breath!"
As if finding themselves back at this terrible point, this

dramatic bridge between birth and death. . . .
But because we do not have an umbilical cord beating for
us, providing us with precious oxygen, the situation
very quickly becomes unbearable . . . for us, that is to
say.
"Do something! Do something!" clamors the unhappy
voice within . . . the voice of our own anxiety.
While the easiest, most sensible thing for us to
do would be to take a deep breath,
instead,
we cut the cord!
The poor victim of this dramatic confusion, this
unconscious projection, abruptly deprived of his
umbilical cord and his previous supply of oxygen,
suddenly finds himself choking to death.
In utter despair, he utters the abominable scream
everyone was so anxiously expecting, which brings
a smile to the faces of . . . the fools we are.
"Ah, he's breathing!" everyone exclaims with great
relief.
"Ah, now *I* can breathe. I'm so relieved," is what
we might say if we were just a little more clear and
aware of what was going on . . . inside.
This process of projecting will now go on endlessly.
And we proudly call it education.

But is birth really so important, one might ask.
It doesn't last long, you could say, compared with
what comes before and after it.
Maybe it's just a nasty moment to get through.
But that is perhaps somewhat glib. After all, there
is another "nasty moment" which, although equally brief,
nonetheless casts a long shadow, and that is death.
Yes, birth and the moments that follow, however few,
will leave a mark for the rest of life.
It is as if we are heading off in the wrong direction,
starting on the wrong foot.
It's like a boat leaving the harbor, with the poor captain
not knowing he has a faulty compass.
This compass, one might say, is
breathing.

7

When we are born we enter the kingdom of breath.
We embark on this endless oscillation which will carry us
through life to deliver us dutifully
into the hands of death.
Breath is the fragile vessel on which we cross this
ocean of life.
Everyone breathes, of course.
One could almost say . . . everything.

But, for us, whether our breathing is free or impaired
makes all the difference.
How many people go through life half-strangled, incapable
of a real sigh?
Much less real laughter?
To live in freedom is to be able to breathe fully, freely.
Which requires a straight back.
That is to say, a spinal column which is free.
Free and supple, lithe, flexible.
And most people go through life with a broomstick for a
spine.
The mentally ill, for instance, are incapable of taking
a full deep breath.
If there is the least blockage along the spine, breathing—
which is the essence of life—is impaired.
The effects will be felt for a lifetime.
In the same way that no two people have the same face, no
two persons breathe in the same manner.
Everyone breathes his own way.
Usually very badly.
In fact, people say,
"I know I am not breathing well. Maybe I could learn."
Some people even try.
But maybe breathing is not something that can be learned.
The way we breathe was established, once and for all,

the moment we were born.
Far better to pay attention to it at that stage.

8

More dangerously, others will say: "Doubtless birth
does mark the child. But life is not a game. It's a
merciless battle. A jungle. So like it or not, you have to be
aggressive."
It is an error to imagine that birth without violence
produces children who are passive, weak, slow.
Quite the contrary.
Birth without violence produces children who are strong,
because they are free, without conflict.
Free and fully awake.
Aggression is not strength. It is the opposite.
Aggression and violence are the masks of weakness,
impotence and fear.
Strength is sure, sovereign and smiling.

But it would be hard to convince the advocates of violence
and aggression of this.
Because they have suffered themselves, their reaction is
to say:
"Life has been hard on me. I've been knocked around and
it's made me what I am. Let it be the same for my
children."
Which is as mean as saying:

"I've suffered. Let them suffer as well."
An eye for an eye.
The dreadful law of reprisal.
The vicious circle of action and reaction.
Leading only to endless misery and suffering.
Surely the best way to ensure that the bitter taste
will linger in our mouths forever.

You'll find it's the same people who say:
"So, women suffer in childbirth. It probably serves them
right."

9

What is it that makes these people so bitter, so angry?
They have not yet forgiven.
Unconsciously, they're still full of hatred for . . .
their own mothers.
It is this hatred which is at the root of all that
led us to the stake, the Inquisition, the Crusades.
All the abominable massacres committed in the name of
king and country, or even God.
This same hatred which is at the root of the feeling
of guilt, the feeling of sin.
Sin! There is no such thing as sin.
So-called sin is nothing but our own blindness and
ignorance.
Our forgetfulness of the panic that is birth for

the child.
As for pain and suffering, it satisfies no God.
If anyone doubts that there is no fatality of pain,
natural childbirth is there to prove it.

10

What more can be said?
Only one thing.
Try.

Everything that has been said is so simple that one
feels embarrassed at having dwelt on it at such length.
Perhaps we have lost our taste for simplicity.
Once we've understood
the point of this whole story,
why don't we try?
Well, it takes . . . a lot of courage.

We also need patience and humility.
We must keep in mind that it is the child's first experience
of life.
As any good teacher knows, there is one sacred right:
the right of the child to experiment and make his own
discoveries.
Yes, patience, humility and silence,
and the awareness that the newcomer is a person we meet
and greet after he has nearly drowned in a storm.

Oh, and of course . . .
Love.
Without love, the delivery room can be perfect, with the right lighting, the walls soundproofed, the bath temperature just right—and the child will still scream.
If there is still any trace of nervousness, any suppressed anger within ourselves, the baby will pick it up immediately.
His judgment is frighteningly acute.
The baby knows everything. All in his own mysterious way. He catches everything, sees right into our hearts, knows the color of our thoughts, and all without language.

11

"There's still something you haven't told us.
what becomes of these children born in silence?
Are they any different from other children?"
"It's something very subtle. You'd have to see for
yourself."
"All the same, can't you try to tell me?"
"We all go through life wearing masks. The mask of
tragedy far more often than the mask of comedy. And it is
this mask of tragedy that you see on the face of most
newborn babies:
their brows knitted and the corners of their little mouths
turned down.
A mask that hides their real face and makes most of them
appear . . . ugly.
Their poor mothers are downcast, since they expected
a 'lovely' baby.
Thank God, there is another mask.
A wide mouth lifted in a smile, with relaxed eyebrows, and
eyes crinkled with pleasure, not to say delight."
"But surely such a mask is never seen on a newborn
baby?"
"You think not? Then why don't you look for
yourself?"

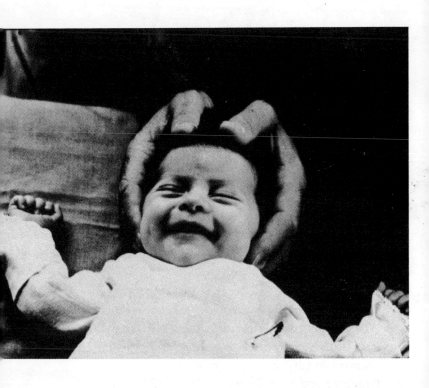

12

"Oh! This baby is really smiling. In fact he's in rapture!"
"It's hard to believe, isn't it?"
"But this picture hasn't got anything to do with what
we've been discussing. The child you're showing me must
be at least three months old.
Babies don't smile before that age."
"That's what people think. People and books.
As for the baby you see before you, he's not even twenty-
four hours old."
"I . . . can't believe it."
"I must admit it's not the image of a newborn baby one is
used to.
And yet, there is still another mask."
"I'm not sure I follow you."
"You might say joy is not better than sorrow. It cannot
last. Both are emotions which, after a while,
cannot but turn into their opposite.
Laughter and tears are very close you know.
Far better not to wear any mask. Far better to be free
of emotions, both good and bad."
"Free . . . of emotions?
Whatever do you mean? I'm not sure I would like that.
And anyway, what's left for us if we don't have our emo-
tions?"
"Well . . ."

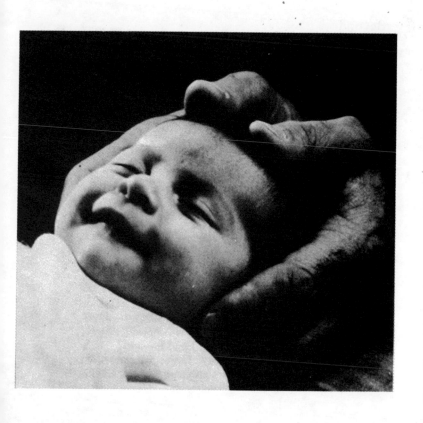

Beyond
tears and laughter,
peace and serenity,
or
as they say in India,

Shanti! Shanti! Shanti!

A Selected List of Cedar Books

While every effort is made to keep prices low, it is sometimes necessary to increase prices at short notice. Mandarin Paperbacks reserves the right to show new retail prices on covers which may differ from those previously advertised in the text or elsewhere.

The prices shown below were correct at the time of going to press.

☐	7493 0938 5	**The Courage to Heal**	Ellen Bass & Laura Davies	£6.99
☐	7493 0046 9	**Sex and Your Health**	James Bevan	£5.99
☐	7493 1611 X	**Food for Healing**	Rachel Charles	£6.99
☐	7493 1544 X	**Mind, Body and Immunity**	Rachel Charles	£6.99
☐	7493 1486 9	**The Alexander Technique**	Judith Leibowitz & Bill Connington	£6.99
☐	7493 2065 6	**Food Fights**	Dr David Haslam	£6.99
☐	7493 1033 2	**The Carbohydrate Addict's Diet**	Dr Rachael Heller & Dr Richard Heller	£6.99
☐	7493 2005 2	**Conceiving Your Baby: How medicine can help**	Sally Keeble	£6.99
☐	7493 0713 7	**Living Together, Feeling Alone**	Dr Dan Kiley	£6.99
☐	7493 0642 4	**Birth Without Violence**	Frederick Leboyer	£6.99
☐	7493 0933 4	**The Amazing Results of Positive Thinking**	Norman Vincent Peale	£6.99
☐	7493 0821 4	**The Power of Positive Living**	Norman Vincent Peale	£6.99
☐	7493 0715 3	**The Power of Positive Thinking**	Norman Vincent Peale	£6.99
☐	7493 1041 3	**How to Survive in Spite of Your Parents**	Dr Margaret Reinhold	£6.99
☐	7493 1955 0	**Beating the Blues**	Xandria Williams	£5.99
☐	7493 2066 4	**Fatigue**	Xandria Williams	£6.99

All these books are available at your bookshop or newsagent, or can be ordered direct from the address below. Just tick the titles you want and fill in the form below.

Cash Sales Department, PO Box 5, Rushden, Northants NN10 6YX.
Fax: 01933 414047 : Phone: 01933 414000.

Please send cheque, payable to 'Reed Book Services Ltd.', or postal order for purchase price quoted and allow the following for postage and packing:

£1.00 for the first book, 50p for the second; **FREE POSTAGE AND PACKING FOR THREE BOOKS OR MORE PER ORDER.**

NAME (Block letters) ....

ADDRESS ....

....

☐ I enclose my remittance for ....

☐ I wish to pay by Access/Visa Card Number

Expiry Date

Signature ....

Please quote our reference: MAND